ON FRIENDSHIP

SAINT JULIAN PRESS

POETRY

Praise for ~ On Friendship

On Friendship is an exquisitely beautiful meditation on love, landscape, and memory. I was transported to distant worlds and reminded of the astonishing meaning to be found in nature and human connection. I loved it ...

—Daniel P. Mason
Assistant Professor in the Department of Psychiatry
at Stanford University and distinguished novelist
whose most recent publication is *North Woods* (2023).

On Friendship is that rare book which travels through centuries and across diverse worlds and histories. It speaks in profound ways to those journeys of the mind forged through deep reflection. Friendship is that central part of one's life which endures in present, past, and future selves. I believe this book will resonate in the hearts and minds of all those fortunate enough to encounter it, long after the last words are read.

—Jayasinhji Jhala
His Highness the *Jhaleshvara* of Dhrangadhra State in Gujarat;
he is also an active film-maker, anthropologist, and historian.

ON FRIENDSHIP

AND THE ORIGINS OF PSYCHE

✠

Kevin McGrath

SAINT JULIAN PRESS
HOUSTON

Published by
SAINT JULIAN PRESS, Inc.
2053 Cortlandt, Suite 200
Houston, Texas 77008

www.saintjulianpress.com

COPYRIGHT © 2024
TWO THOUSAND AND TWENTY-FOUR
©Kevin McGrath

Print ISBN-13: 978-1-955194-23-5
EPUB ISBN-13: 978-1-955194-24-2
Library of Congress Control Number: 2023949255

Cover Art Credit: Constantine Manos © 1972
Courtesy of Magnum Photos
Author Photo Credit: Akos Szilvasi

To V. H. L. B.

*Without friendship there is no memory and
without memory there is no durable light ...*

CONTENTS

I~I ... Argument ... *1*

I~II ... Understanding ... *6*

I~III ... Hellespont ... *15*

II~I ... Hydra ... *26*

II~II ... Maleas ... *42*

II~III ... Odysseus ... *77*

III~I ... Windward ... *86*

III~II ... Kacch ... *113*

III~III ... Amity ... *133*

IV~I ... Winter ... *144*

IV~II ... King ... *153*

IV~III ... Terminus ... *165*

INTRODUCTION

ON FRIENDSHIP is a book about the origins of consciousness and the place that *friendship* possesses in that process. As early human beings advanced out of Africa and slowly populated our earth they did so in terms of walking. Friendship, more than any other emotional experience—rather than kinship—was central in that development of incipient awareness. The practice of walking was a condition that was profoundly inherent in the early composition of psyche and this book presents four *Walks*—in Greece, the Windward Isles, western India, and New England—as representative of such apprehension. Walking is here portrayed as a transcendental and philosophical activity and as a constitutive source—through the work of apperception—of human understanding. It is the development of friendship that transformed the experience of the pedestrian from one of the most intrinsic sources of the human psyche into a situation of moral sentience.

—Kevin McGrath

ON FRIENDSHIP

~ On Friendship ~

I ~ I

FRIENDSHIP lies at the heart of what it means to be human, in terms of person, place, and ultimately, in terms of that devotion which has no object. By *friendship* I mean an affinity which we elect and not the profoundly driven nor compulsive love that charges us with complex sexual fervor, a behaviour that only reiterates itself. Friendship in this sense is not evolutionary nor biological but is founded upon the mobility of humanistic attraction which is both indelible and admirable.

Obversely, to be human is to experience grief, for loss is the most foundational and generative act of our emotional life. The conditions of friendship overlay this situation of a deficiency of sentiment, for unlike human love sorrow is immediate and unequivocal and is not born out of physiological imperative. Friendship always recognises signs of grief, those aspects of a person which are composed of absence, the wordless affective hollows that have been received from life, empty vessels which we bear with us throughout time. Animals arguably do not experience grief, they can know distress and anxiety but grief is an especially human emotion which is not a component of animal affect. Such creatures, of course, have no anticipation nor conceptual knowledge of death.

From a more social dimension, the mutual aid of human co-operation rather than the competition of worldly contest is one of the fundamental paradigms of our mortal and admiring psyche, how it is that we collaborate and conjoin in our efforts and feelings in order to accomplish collective residence here on earth. Allied to this view is the idea of the *commons*, either conceptually or materially, being a locative situation upon which or in which a community shares both work and station. The notion of a survival of the fittest is only applicable genetically, where the species with the best material disposition will triumph for a while; it is social co-operation which occurs among communities within a species that causes success in a natural sense.

Altruism is the nature of this ground, that goodness which occurs among companions which partakes of no forceful hierarchy and which attempts to foresee the benefit of another. We are refined by altruism and so become gracious in an amicable fashion and this condition allows us to look or to go beyond our worldly self.

Animals co-operate and can behave altruistically and yet there is no friendship amongst creatures; they work together during hunting or during the infancy of their offspring and there is courtship and reproduction but no friendship between wild *fauna*. Amity is a particularly and uniquely human characteristic, what I would assert as the most humane of all hominid features and most intrinsic to the natural generation of psyche or consciousness.

Let us examine certain iterations of this proposition from three dimensions, concerning the presence of human amity and its psychic agency in our brief and fragile lives.

Firstly, it is the assistance and co-ordination which occurs between two individuals that causes the substance of what I would consider to be friendship, a communal and reciprocal understanding of another whom one admires. There is simultaneously a perception of the beautiful as a crucial focal element within this emotional movement of the human within a *milieu* of territorial attachment, where a landscape supports a companionable and human bond. By beautiful here I would imply the morally and not the materially beautiful.

Our admiration for places is a most ancient experience and necessary for the ongoing sustenance of both humanity and the natural world, however with dense and irreverent urbanisation such equilibrium with physical topography and its seasonal variation of sources often no longer obtains. This quality of topographic company is something which can be recapitulated by the walker, the pedestrian who, passing through a rare wilderness alone or in company, so retrieves an earlier mode of consciousness or what I would call *psyche* in the abstract. In this sense amity for place and for person possess similar aetiologies in that they both glimpse the nakedness of an inherent and usually undisclosed beauty.

Going one step further, it is the elective comprehension which one offers towards the *kosmos* itself, that universal perception which in the end allows us to exist in a manner that is not solitary but complete and without any quality that is individual; for apperception can indeed become a cause of knowledge. It was the longing of the hero Achilles for what he understood as the transcendence of poetry which enacted his passion, or, the yearning of the mariner Odysseus for a vision of his natal terrain, wife, and son, an ideal belief that sustained his inner sense of direction for almost a decade of desperately metonymical wandering, interspersed with many verbal *duets* during which time he harvested the means of travel.

Psyche in this sense is like a puissant compass needle that mysteriously directs our way. Evolution initially impels this psychic agency, then, all that we receive from life and the world mimetically amplifies this record of the recipient, and eventually there is the indistinct quality of election which moves such consciousness further in the direction of friendship for place and person. Yet it is not that we elect but that we are driven to be elected, and this is the most distinct, profound, and unspeakable instant that marks the kind of alliance which I am portraying in this book: evinced by the four walks and a swim that are depicted on the ensuing pages, each representing a different kind of amicable model and its *mimésis*, ambition, or teleological sources.

Secondly, friendship is a reticulation which supports our life in terms of the personal, the topographical, and the supernal. In the following pages such kinds of appreciation and transition—the mnemonics and vicissitudes of such goodwill—are presented and portrayed, describing the various *rapports* which surround and inform our days, some of which are passed with companions and others which are experienced with affection and attachment directed toward natural geography and the locative. All these passages concern crossings of sorts, movements from one to another which are fundamentally typified by the perpetual east-west transit of the great sun itself.

We mentor and are mentored and this amorphous and unannounced activity lies at the fount of our kind understanding on earth. Ultimately every human being is faced with the question of possible perfection and absolute void and how we are to apprehend that final and undisclosed yet necessary dilemma. It is imperative that we accomplish this state of our last traverse in a condition of attraction and ideal amity if we are to be harmonious on earth; for it is not what we leave behind but what we go toward that counts in the end.

Thirdly, if ambulant and persistent migration is one of the most profound modes within both animal and human consciousness then the impulse for both movement and for pause derives from human kinship towards place and person, and how the psychic moves in terms of verbal migration is a similar quality of the transitive. Just as our initial seconds of awareness ascend out of sleep or grief so too the kinetic human mind most truly arises from affinity and not from biology: anatomy is not destiny. It is the demonstration and knowledge of such unique attachments that remain with us in the end, dramatised by our conception and esteem of vital and myriad beauty; for our perception of ephemeral beauty is the *eikon* which first catches our hearts.

Walking and amiable conversation are arranged and orchestrated according to this most fundamental currency of natural, terrestrial, and moral affinity which underpins so much of our synoptic belief in the world; for as we first evolved towards awareness and language our medium of days was only pedestrian. Human migration was always subject to these orders which in an historical sense devised our first evolutionary modes and which later became integral forms of moral consciousness: moments of psyche that are the media of all recipience, or that which most signally informs our earthly standing. Human migration about the planet is one of our most ancient mental paradigms and how the footloose migrant finds equilibrium within a physical terrain; how he or she establishes a life amongst those who are already resident is realised by an act of friendship and moral reciprocity.

Ultimately and irrefutably there is that enigmatic condition of discrete election, an action which entails continuities rather than entities: not how one determines but how one is determined. This eventual point is the terminus of our present literal trajectory.

I ~ II

UNDERSTANDING what it means to be human goes further than simply living the life of a practical humanist, that is, of someone who attempts to comprehend what he or she is not. Understanding concerns a movement both among and within language for that is our only vehicle here on earth apart from those rare occasions of sublimity or transcendence when the experience of an uncommon landscape, of a work of art, or even of the affection of another human being touches us unspeakably.

All these circumstances partake of a certain nakedness, a psychic nudity where nothing hinders or covers over our living envelope of person. Such words however, bear their own conventions and convey their own cargo as they cannot become ours to individually possess, that is the dilemma; for if we are to truly understand we need to secure another medium so that consciousness might acquire both support and sustenance.

Recently I was attending a midday recital of organ music at the little monastery that is adjacent to the river here in Cambridge. I must have fallen asleep—although I was aware of listening to all of the programme—for suddenly it was as if I was visually witnessing my life move quickly past and before me as if upon a child's Nineteenth-century lantern-slide showing.

Images of southern China and of the low hills and littoral of my childhood were there as were pictures of sailing offshore from rocky Welsh Anglesey in my youth; there were views of Pragsar in the Kacch of Gujarat where I have so often walked about the desert and of the Chari Dhand where I once spent days among the migrant birds. There were images from the mid-Atlantic during one of my crossings and scenes from the southern Sudan and the Red Sea reef of Sangeneb, but most of all there was one especial image taken from Lakonia in the southern Peloponnese where I had often sauntered. That particular picture, of all those images which passed before me during the recital when my eyes were closed, for some reason assumes a prominence and valence which none of the other pictures own, for it remains curiously unique. In fact, those profound minutes have assumed a presence in my consciousness and are unlike any other experience which I possess.

Most of those rare experiences that emerged and disappeared during the recital came from pedestrian activity which for me has always held a moral purpose. Swimming, in lakes or ocean is sometimes akin to this and the swim can become a work of art. Once, making passages under sail held a similar transformative agency for me although nowadays my life at sea is a quality only of the past and I pursue aquatic ideals through rowing, here on the Charles River.

All this kind of experience is merely a mode that enables one to transcend away from the mundane and diurnal and to approach a condition that is fully replete with a potential of visionary excess. Even once, when down on lonely Maleas I one morning found myself transported upwards in a second of supernal consciousness so that it was possible to perceive the lucid and spherical *kosmos* from an altitude, even that sovereign occasion does not possess the wholeness, harmony, or radiance of those few times when I would pause at a cistern for water as I walked the Lakonic coast.

Of all those images that appeared to me that noon-time this single occasion stands perfectly apart and stationary; it occurred during a particular walk that I did many times and is distinct from all those other fleeting reminiscences that came to me whilst listening to a performance of the *Well-Tempered Klavier*. That one instant, which even now I have before me as a vivid sight, happened at a small tank where I often rested on the walk in order to throw a bucket down into the water and to drink; or, if it was extremely hot and bright, I would strip off my shorts and sandals and douse myself, rinsing the white powdery sand of the day's journey from my skin.

The covered cistern was about half-way on a long sixty kilometre journey between an upland village called Richea and a house south of Monembasia in the coastal province of Sparta. I would set out in the early morning, going downhill through several miles of antique olive groves and on reaching the old late-Mycenaean port of Zarax turn south and proceed along the coast, taking a path which was thick with hot printless dust. Due to the solitary cistern I never carried a water bottle, an item which one otherwise always needed when wandering afoot in meridian Greece.

Why that particular point of the walk stays with me so strongly and exclusively—more than any other image drawn from life—is difficult to explain or to understand. How is one to justify the strength and exception of that mental circumstance and what made it so outstanding or honest?

It was not that those days of strolling were so carefree, for they were definitely not that, nor was it that I was happy then. I actually consider happiness not to be a salient pursuit in life—unlike how it is expressed in the American Constitution which pronounces this feeling to be both a human right and an ethical imperative—and believe that there are other and far more vital transactions or intentions in time which can be identified and tracked and perhaps achieved: like one's apprehension of the beautiful, or of the nature and character of numinous truth, or of enduring goodness. That unspoken and solitaire incident beside the cistern was a moment of benign weightlessness, an occasion where all the metaphors that enclose our lives were briefly discharged and one could stand undressed, as it were, in the sunlight and alone for miles, being merely pedestrian and lightly thoughtless upon the dry grainy earth and yet being concurrently super-conscious.

There is also the aspect of *love of place* which for me has always been of equal stature to *love of person*, both are equally paradigms of *philía*. I so adored that area about Zarax, its bare and overt antiquity and its lack of anything humane apart from a few goat pens, the olive and fig trees, the sage, thyme, and the glittering and empty turquoise ultramarine that touched the coast. Above the tiny and hidden port of Zarax, up within the old grey walls of the citadel which had once guarded and overseen that diminutive harbour, I had one afternoon discovered a small black obsidian arrow-head beside those great stones, walls built of gigantic and smooth grey rock, each one of several tons in mass and most cleanly mortised.

I had walked far in Lakonia, sometimes for many weeks, sleeping out in uninhabited places and on those unpeopled shores. It is difficult to communicate that kind of passion, a passion for terrain and topography, for a landscape which was profoundly imbued with millennia of human proficiency, although presently all that involvement was now absent except for those ancient walls or the occasional painted potsherd or my handsome little glassy arrow-head.

If amity is an experience of unworldly joy, of being that is free of encumbrance, an emotion that exists only in an outgoing which is without reception, my minutes of pausing beside that cistern were certainly perhaps the most joyous event in my life. Looking back in retrospection, those days must have taken place in the Summer of Nineteen Eighty-Five, which, given my age now is a point that is exactly midway through my earthly duration.

From another perspective, I have devoted many years to the study of ancient heroes, particularly those of the Homeric world and those of the Sanskrit epic Mahabharata. For me there is no more perfect work of art than the Homeric Iliad, nothing equals that, to my knowledge: not in painting, sculpture, in music, nor architecture, for Iliad is unique in its near-absolute integrity and magnificent extent. Strangely, the Homeric Odyssey is not like that, not for me, for it is evasive, irrational, super-complex, and completely inexplicable in its arrangement of narrative order. No matter how many times I reread this poem I still cannot understand its frames and perspective and moreover, I cannot even comprehend why it is so elusive: what should that indicate for us as readers today and what is the project so hidden by this countenance, for such a fashion of anti-structure is almost inhuman. Nevertheless, like Odysseus I had once with a companion tacked a tender white ketch into the bay of Kykladic Pholegandros during a stormy yet sparkling *meltemi*, barely slipping between the rocks which guard that port, and thus I do claim to understand with a slight mimetic expertise something of that unbreakable poem's physical panorama.

Decades of examining the literature of those late bronze age heroes and especially the brief sojourn of radiant Achilles, have likewise provided me with an understanding of what it is to perceive—like him—of how we might view the insufferable nature of being timeless and how the emotions respond to such a prospect. The complexity and sophistication and yet the ease of poetry in Homeric Iliad are virtually equal to the irrefutable properties of nature itself and that vision of young Achilles as he stands upon the plain before Troy is an outlook which is tantamount to true promise. The conclusive grief of this youthful warrior is composed by a coincident presence and absence, the absolute loss and wonderful potential of his *refusal*.

There is no hero with the vision of Achilles and it is as if he is thoroughly without metaphor, such is his terrific view of the *kosmos*, and hence the inordinate and unbearable sorrow which imbues every second of his brief life. Even the supernatural is a daily familiar of Achilles and yet this beautiful sanguine charioteer becomes aware, impossibly aware, that when his friend perishes even the immortal bearing of human poetry might also become subject to the similarly total demise of invincible extinction.

In the same style, countless seasons of slowly reading the words of the Sanskrit heroes of the Great Bharata have conduced to my firm interpretation of preliterate and premonetary culture three thousand years ago in North-West India. The doubling cognition and mnemonic workings of those poets, how they were inspired both acoustically and visually and how it was that they portrayed moral authority, femininity, and most importantly, how they knew the custom and intricacies of natural life, the aerial and telluric: all these psychic mechanisms are conveyed in that most archaic of poems with an extraordinary and circular implication. Most significant is the knowledge which those poets acquired from the exertion of *dhyana* or 'profound reflection', an activity which correspondingly lies at the core of my own professional sentience: how one marks victory in the face of annihilation when prolific death is the sole adamantine yet unifying criterion.

Similarly, the act of *writing* poetry, which has been the course of my life for half a century now, has brought to me a kind of *under*-standing of the circulating universe. This has been not so much an achievement in the production of certain objects or works but of having momentary access to a phenomenal medium which translates one toward a particular apprehension: the evidential awareness of more than mortal being. Poetry has been simply a pathway, an unbelievably and incredibly difficult trajectory where one's balance, discipline, resolution, and tenacity, have allowed sightless footsteps to be made in an unequivocally certain direction toward an aim which one knows but which cannot be in any manner made materially manifest or immediate.

In this case the work produces nothing that is really of value, there is no worth nor consequence and yet the process itself is wholly valuable and worthy, for without that course there would be no movement nor temporal division. In that sense poetry or the writing of poetry is like walking, it being one of the most ancient of human activities and yet it is only a state of transmission and never a feature of objective invention or fabrication.

The vicissitudes of human affection or what people in our Western world commonly refer to as *love* likewise might possess or supply us with understanding. This is not a situation of genitality nor of feasible partnering but of being that offers to another more than it receives from another; that is what I mean by amity. For Proust, who, like Dante, was a masterly cartographer of human necessity—its moods, affinities, compulsion and repulsion—love was an experience of eminent recollection or *recherche* in which the incidence of retrospection was actually greater than the original experience itself; for it was only within that reverse view or assessment which was removed from time that Marcel was able to grasp and to understand literally the truth of his life.

Ironically, not one of his figures ever successfully loves for they are all in pursuit asymptotically, and not one character—certainly not Swann nor the author himself with Albertine—was ever to secure any stability of affection. Such is the paradox which *maestro* Proust evinces and his genius makes overt that agonising yet oblivious and impulsive solitude of the human, an activity that is over-played by such perpetual questing for what can only be in fact an interminably hypothetical ideal of personal union.

What is it that causes a young man to approach a young woman with a gift, or *vice-versa*, and what is it that is really about to be exchanged in that meeting and perhaps embrace? This is not simply biological magnetism nor the drama of sexual attraction and selection, nor are such events merely transferential, where one unconscious narrative combines with another in order to advance towards an ever-retreating point of synthetic closure. Some other conduit is at work and it is this which Proust was able to capture in his prolonged record, something that by nature is permanently at one protracted remove, a plateau whereupon we become just vehicles, vacant pronouns in desperate need of adjectives, themselves impelled to secure verbs and adverbs; yet there are no real objects nor gains only further sentence and subjection. In this sense our knowledge of time and transition is only constituted of infinite metonymy and transitory terminus can only be acquired—like victory for an athlete in a race—by an act of conceptual slowness or of pause. The foundation of marital fidelity participates in that same refractive lightness.

In literature one can always distinguish between 'plot' or *muthos*, and 'story' or *praxéos*, where the former concerns a sequence of causal events and the latter demonstrates a series of temporal measures. It is the former, in terms of human life, which renders understanding, if one is able to discern that progression of moments which link up the process of how it is that we exist or have existed. To understand, in this case, is to dramatise or to cause such a display of succession to occur, which is another way of stating the tragic, where realisation and awareness are suddenly constellated and that immanence encompassing human loss becomes momentarily activated.

Sometimes architecture can provide one with such a view, as once when I was with a friend and visiting Chiswick House on the edge of London, it was as if we were unexpectedly being held and contained or framed within the planes and perfectly proportioned surfaces inside which we stood, as if they were sensibly replicating the ratios and dimension of the universe itself. Held within that transparent and weightless pattern of faultless architectural dimension for a few seconds one could perceive something that was being perfectly and completely implied.

Ultimately it is to such friends that I offer my gratitude, not primarily to places nor to certain beloved individuals, but to the long-standing companions who have been confident and amicable in this life. This recognition is not simply a valediction for affection, conversation, or for intellectual exchange but for the fact that I have spent a great part of my life *thinking* about them with admiration and trying to understand them for what I am not and how it was that they thought of worldly creation and of humane living. This is the only true or worthwhile intimacy insofar as it conducts us toward our most genuine conception.

It is this long and careful reflection which has truly introduced me to the nature of understanding and without them I would never have found myself standing beside that cistern and throwing an old and galvanised zinc bucket into the depths in order to drink and assuage a thirst. These are the *friends*, those who remain with one even when we are completely isolated and apart from life, and without their unseen presence we cannot drink nor can we even remember.

There are other dimensions and facets that amplify and magnify this kind of musical understanding and it is as if we were actually and in fact understanding the immutable sky or heaven with its stars, meteors, comets, constellations, and galaxies, from which we earth-beings have been generated and descended and which—in their elliptical and never linear motion—continue to influence and inform our terrestrial and affective lives.

Those minutes, those few occasions when I halted beside that cistern, were in retrospect the zenith of my life, my midsummer-apex as it were when I stood closest to the Sun, momentarily undressed of all language and even of belief; for having received that most indelible gift of human amity I could then experience the true pleasure of being without words.

~ ON FRIENDSHIP ~

I ~ I I I

DURING the course of the recent decades I have made a series of long walks, some of them of many days' duration. They took place in Greece, Africa, India, Britain, and America, and supplied the conceptual ground for much of my written work. As a continuation of this model one summer long ago I swam the Hellespont, the enclosed stretch of water between the continents of Asia and Europe. That swim for me was very much a work of art and concerned consciousness more than anything simply aquatic.

I made the swim in imitation of Byron who himself was imitating the Leandros of myth. In that account, Leandros would each night swim from Asian Abydos across the channel in order to be with his beloved Hero, a priestess of Aphrodite at Sestos. Leandros ultimately drowned one stormy evening and Hero in despair threw herself into the waters. The myth was made English by the poem of Christopher Marlowe and included the famed line, "Who ever lov'd, that lov'd not at first sight?" Byron, in one of his letters, commented that Leandros, "swam for Love, as I for Glory."

The Hellespont is one of the narrowest passages of water between the masses of Asia and Europe, although Turkey now extends its frontier well into the western side. It is so called because there, Helle fell from the Golden Ram— and hence Fleece—as it flew northwards across the sky towards Colchis. It was where Xerxes on his way to invade Greece in 480 B.C.E. built his renowned bridge of boats. Because the sea eventually destroyed the bridge Xerxes ordered that the waters be beaten with whips in punishment. Alexander also traversed this point in 334. Until Byzantium was established as a trading *entrepôt* in the early centuries of the Common Era the Hellespont was the station of all major traffic between the East and the West.

I arrived at the town of Canakkale on the afternoon of the twenty-third of July having made my way, *via* the island of Lesbos, from Athens. Canakkale is just north of the great plain of the Troad, site of Homeric Troy where Achilles had walked and sung. Just south of Canakkale was where the Allied forces had assayed to land in 1915 during a horribly fatal campaign organised by Churchill. The Dardanelles memorial stood further down the coast on the European side and recalled the death of at least a quarter of a million young men. There was also a Turkish memorial a little further along the shore, remembering their tens of thousands who had fallen.

I had been travelling for two days when I arrived and was tired and hungry and I intended to find a small *pension* and rest and then to make a preliminary reconnaissance the next day. A strong etesian wind was blowing and the waters of the channel were rough—too troubled to swim—which was rather distressing for me. Although I had lived for many years in Greece and considered myself genuinely Philhellenic it was wonderful to be back on the Turkish shore with its whiff of Asia and the steppe. The topography was different and the land was dotted with minarets and poplars and was certainly a margin of the Orient. Fortuitously, as I strolled into the *Capitainerie* to look at a nautical chart pinned to a wall, I met someone who was soon to become my agent: Aydogan Enginer. He was to arrange all the practical aspects of the swim, including the finding of a boatman, an old mariner called Zafir, whose *caique* accompanied us across the strait.

For many years I had been making walks off into empty landscapes, generally on paths and tracks and away from human settlement. Landscape for me was something far more than the picturesque, it was a situation of thought and essential component to my poetry. Indeed, the pastoral has been a vital theme in Western poetry since classical times when idyllic verse had praised rural *locale* for its natural and benign qualities. It was a place for ideal affection, for uncomplicated simplicity, benevolence, innocence, and therefore truthful amity. Even in Sanskrit poetry—and I am a scholar by profession and spend a great deal of my life closely reading Sanskrit epic—nature was conceived as something ethically pure and not at all savage; it was somewhere essentially harmonious towards which to retreat at an appropriate season in life.

My walks over the years, many of them in southern Greece, had been attempts at securing some vision or realisation of this ideal and were attempts to move away from the finite and mundane. They had to be slow and the vista empty and the walk was an occasion for a progress away from the merely temporal. Solitude had been a key element in these journeys. I had also walked in East Africa—foolishly, as it turned out—and in western India, in the Kacch, in what was virtually desert. Walks in Scotland and Wales lay farther off in the background, for that was where, as a youthful scholar, I had really begun to make these mental forays.

For the Romantics, and Byron was one of their elite, landscape played a crucial philosophical role, especially as it concerned the sublime. Nature from this perspective was a counterpoint to the urban and rational world of the Enlightenment and its nascent industrialisation and terrain was not only a locus of beauty but also of *veritas*, offering a possibility for transcendence. For the Romantics, landscape supplied a reality more potential and profound than that available elsewhere and their written testaments of such experience were supposed to effect a further transformation in the reader or audience. It was a movement, intellectually speaking, that was a child of the American and French revolutions, discovering in natural solitude a freedom and liberty denied to political society.

The *Prelude* of William Wordsworth fully describes the form of some of these influences, where, through an intense scrutiny of the intrinsic qualities of a district, Wordsworth sought to make overt its otherworldly dimension: *via* a means of emotional detachment which allowed the articulation of such undersigned forms. Friendship among the Romantics was a crucial and dynamic element that underlay all their individual and aesthetic endeavours and the work of Wordsworth was profoundly informed by conversation and strolling with his friend Sam Coleridge.

In much of the West today nature is confined and maintained in 'parks', that is, within artificial boundaries, whereas for the Romantics, nature was the archetype of freedom and the unconstrained. Many of them had been extreme democrats and devoted to radical principles and a few of them had often been driven into exile and were akin to what in the Twentieth century would be termed an *avant-garde*. Byron himself, because of his ideals and also due to his sexual disposition, had fled London and died in 1824 engaged in the Greek struggle for independence. Percy Shelley, his best companion, had similarly to depart from English shores because of his belief in atheism and free love; in his poetry, literary landscape offered a world where memory and metaphysical anticipation could converge. He was to drown later, sailing off Italy with a friend.

So there I was in Canakkale, weary from my journey as I had barely eaten in two days, yet tense and charged with the impetus of having to somehow accomplish this swim. In Cambridge I had been sculling all spring on the Charles and then in southern Greece I had been swimming for many hours each day, usually in high seas, in preparation for the crossing, so I was physically well prepared. I had expected all kinds of delays and problems, with weather, bureaucracy, and the finding of a boat to assist me, but none of this happened. Even before I had managed to eat or rest, I was with Zafir and Aydogan and motoring out towards the low headland just north of Canakkale where ancient Abydos once stood.

Leandros had made this swim nightly from Abydos to Sestos, to Hero in her tower. Byron, along with a naval *confidant*, had attempted his swim in the spring of 1810 and had failed due to the impetuosity and coldness of the sea; a second attempt soon after succeeded. In a letter to England he had written, "I plume myself on this achievement more than I could possibly do on any kind of glory, political, poetical, or rhetorical." Now my own chance had suddenly arrived.

As the little fishing *caique*, the *Döstler*, which means 'Friendship', motored up towards Abydos, I sat in the stern trying to focus on what was happening. When I first encountered Aydogan and we had begun talking I told him of my plan and he laughed, saying how preposterous it was. Then we had sat down in the shade out on the quai and drunk cold water and discussed the problem. "Well," he said, "it is possible, but difficult. Permits are needed, they take months, and it is dangerous if the police find out, but let me see." Soon my foreign currency was being passed over the table and Aydogan had gone off to find his comrade Zafir. They returned in about an hour and a few fisherman assembled to cheer and clap as we set off. By then I had begun to feel both imprudent and grandiose.

Fortunately the wind had dropped. As in Greece, these strong summer winds only blow during the day and as the sun nears the horizon, they diminish. Twilight was soon to be upon us as we proceeded and as we approached the promontory of Abydos I could discern that it was now a highly fortified military base with massive artillery emplacements capable of dominating access to and from the Black Sea. It was a sinister and totally silent prospect, for despite all the signs of an army, no human was apparent; I almost expected a patrol boat to dash out or to hear a warning shot. Aydogan indicated the sites where three Allied battleships, sunk during the Dardanelles campaign, now lay; the depth below us was well in excess of an hundred fathoms.

The Hellespont marks the spot where the waters, draining from the Black Sea, rush out toward the Aegean; also, as it is the narrowest point between the continents this current is strong and irregular. This I was prepared for, knowing that my actual course would not be the direct mile and a half, but rather a curve of possibly several miles; what I had not planned for were jellyfish, and worse, the tankers.

Walking had always presented its spectrum of problems, the main one often being how to obtain sufficient water. Snakes had also sometimes caused difficulties, or scorpions when I had been sleeping out on the ground, and once in the southern Sudan I had found a scorpion inside my sleeping bag. Wild dogs had caused my worst experience on two other walks. None of those intrusions had been at all sublime, rather, they had supplied an element of threat and disorder that was far from ideal. Now, however, I had to somehow skirt these gigantic and fast moving tankers, especially the south-bound ones which had the benefit of a swift current of several knots under them. This was why Zafir had been involved, and why Aydogan had very cleverly provided himself with a whistle.

After dropping off some supplies with one of Zafir's friends—an old man who was fishing—we ran in close to the shore beneath the camouflaged guns and idled in the shallows. I had by then changed into swimming trunks and was feeling tense, not at all genial nor romantic. Originally, I had intended to swim naked but discreet inquiries with Zafir made me realise that this would be perceived as immodest. We quietly sat watching the ships as they passed up and down the strait, timing their passage. After a while I gave up, and Aydogan and I began to talk about Turkey's entry to the EU.

Suddenly I felt the boat swing round and Zafir shouted, "GO!" I remembered to say "Bismillah," an invocation to Allah, and without further thought dived over the side and immediately began swimming with a fast pace. I then settled to a slower and more steady rate as a flight of terns, low and shadowy, flew close before me going north. The sea was warm and comfortable and its motion agreeable, until jellyfish began to pass over my body, a sensation that was profoundly unpleasant and disturbing but which I forced myself to disregard. Then came the first of the tankers.

It was only two months later, when I was sailing in Boston harbour with friends, that I was to realise how frightening those ships had really been. At the time I was so intent on the swim that I completely denied the terror that they presented. During the yacht race the boat had been flying a spinnaker, which meant that any directional change was a complex proposition. We had just come round the back of an island—with which Boston harbour is well-provided—when a tanker appeared steaming surely into port. We quickly changed course and passed close beneath the stern of the vessel across a deep and extremely turbulent wake and were forced to inhale a stink of diesel fumes. Only at that moment did the awful and horrible fear return to me, of how terrific those steel leviathans had been in the Dardanelles. It was as if suddenly I was back in the water and it was only at that moment—long after the event itself—that I was actually aware of what I had experienced. During the swim I had simply ignored that intense *angst* and felt no fear at all.

Without Zafir being there to gauge the distances the expedition would not have been successful, and Aydogan blew his whistle when he needed to inform me of a change in course or speed. We proceeded to cross what was the busiest and narrowest shipping lane in the world, at first without any problems, timing the course of the vessels with ease. With my head only inches out of the water and in fading light, no officer on a bridge could have possibly observed me down there.

Then came the good ship *Congratulation* from Socotra, a nice title, given my situation. We miscalculated and I was close enough to wave at some seamen on deck who gathered astonished at the sight. The wash from the propellers was troublesome as was the odour of fuel and I could hear a deep slow thrumming of engines. Friends in Greece had kindly warned me to beware of the force generated by the screws and the danger of being sucked down into a vortex; long ago in the bay of Paros an acquaintance had perished like that.

There were a couple of other close encounters and then we really had a problem when one fast-moving vessel came bearing down on us and we completely mistimed the track. Zafir turned the boat back and gunned the motor and Aydogan furiously blew his whistle. By then I was almost able to count the rivets on the hull of the ship and to inspect its portholes. It was the only instant where I felt that I was possibly in serious trouble and I even briefly considered climbing back into the *Döstler*. That moment also passed however and we resumed the crossing.

Soon the shipping lanes were behind us and the rest was easy and pleasurable and I even contemplated swimming back. By then the low slopes of the European continent were visible in detail, covered in olive groves and gentle declivity. I thought of Leandros and his beloved, and of Byron and his friend and their triumph. Ahead I could discern the ruins, not of Hero's tower but of some low Ottoman fortification. How tranquil the land looked in the dusk with a young apricot-coloured moon setting over the hills, and near it, almost within its thin white arms, the planet Venus; I could also hear the rasping hiss of the last of the day's cicadas. On the eastern side of the channel lights were coming on and Canakkale was already a mass of small yellow brilliants. That was a happy moment for me.

I could hear Zafir cutting the revs and readying his anchor chain as I swam up to the shore in order to touch the bottom with my toes. I then returned to the boat and climbed aboard. Aydogan was busying himself making a cup of tea on a small primus stove and cutting open a water-melon. Zafir was in trunks and putting on a mask and snorkel and went over the side and soon started throwing mussels into the boat, which Aydogan began to cook in a pot. Music was issuing from a little radio.

As darkness came the three of us were sitting happily drinking raki and chatting. I soon drifted off into my own meditations, thinking of Byron and what he had written about this region. When he had passed this way there had been no roads, a few tracks here and there, no wires, no engines and very few people about the land. Those days had been the happiest moments of his life in terms of friendship and geniality, when he had been a resident in Athens and then during his journey up towards Istanbul, just north of here. I thought of how very fortunate I was in meeting with my own good companions.

The next morning, as I made my back towards Greece and south into the province of Lakonia where I then lived, I began to reformulate those experiences: that is what interested me, the concept of the swim and not merely its accomplishment. For me the theoretical aspect was just as signifying as the physical and I began to abstract and sift my feelings and recollections for further meaning.

That summer I had turned fifty and I had wanted to symbolise the transition—the crossing of a mid-century—by some material act. Also, as an Indologist, my professional life was spent in adaptation and explication of what Eastern literature meant to the West, and the Dardanelles had always been, for millennia, a critical point of translation between Orient and Occident. Further, I had just completed a cycle of thought which I had been working on for over sixteen years, then called *Maleas*, in which my various walks had been represented and organised in terms of *idea*. Those walks had enabled me to cultivate an experience that had not been perceptible in a daily or social setting and had supplied me with the sufficient condition for a work of art, the poem, as well as drawing me closer to certain friends.

My last important walk had been down on the very southern end of Lakonia, towards the Cape of Maleas. It was near this headland that Odysseus had been blown off course during his return voyage: "he should have gone home at that time unharmed, had not the north wind and the currents been against him as he was doubling Cape Maleas," said the poets. On one of my walks during the early Eighties I had spent over forty days on that peninsula, patrolling the hills and coast, often simply in search of the brackish water only to be found in abandoned cisterns. Maleas had a curious tendency to disorient and to test and one easily became lost down there, in every sense of the word.

That journey had been the most important walk that I had ever achieved and I had spent the next decade and a half writing about it, reforming the experience in terms of poetry. In a sense, it was only *after* the event, in the mental recession from actual time, that one could truly comprehend what had occurred and then be able to express the experience as a poetic fiction. Byron too had conceived and refined, *via* language, his experience of swims, rides, and sea journeys, in verse and letters: *Childe Harold*, was a poem very much concerned with the intersection of geography and liberty. The Hellespont swim was, for me, a mark of conclusion to that original walk down on Cape Maleas sixteen years earlier, and in effect, its final component and the thoughts which were generated during that long retreat about Maleas culminated in the swim. By virtue of that transit, with all its mythical dimensions, the crossing had provided both the necessary and sufficient closure to my book.

It had been a swim not only in a practical sense but for me had dramatised during its two hours—and I am not sure exactly how long it had taken as I had forgotten to check my wristwatch—a reconnection with something larger and atemporal. During that interval, I was briefly moving away from the usual categories of reflection, which brought in its wake both the beautiful and the threatening. This was an experience only to be formally measured out in subsequent writing. It had not been simply a replay of an earlier poetic event—modernism amplifying romanticism, which itself attempted to recreate the paradigm of earlier myth—but an effort to seize upon an idea. The marine landscape, with its intense intimacy and uniqueness, had been simultaneously deeply resonant and troubling.

Mimésis was a key element to this kind of thinking: an imitation of myth for Byron, and an imitation of an historical event, for me; Leandros had been in love and his heroic passion had overwhelmed him. Byron had been a frequently melancholic man, struggling throughout life with his own extraordinary genius and its concomitant inability to achieve any satisfying and reciprocal affection: that was to be always evasive. His traverse of the Hellespont had supplied him with a brief instant of triumph as well as providing him with a means to overcome physical disability, lameness due to a club-foot. This was his most perfect metaphor. He had been able, *via* the swim, to re-conceptualise that division between the physical and the ideal, through an imitation of *myth*, and there he had secured an access to both the beautiful and unlimited.

Re-enactment of myth nearly always brings with it a condition of heightened emotion, this is what makes ritual efficacious. Classicism, as a *genre*, projects a system of orders, whereas romanticism rejects that syntax of law in favour of greater immediacy, it is more phenomenal. Modernism and expressionism are direct heirs respectively to these aesthetic positions, with their corollaries of individual and linguistic alienation. As a creature of the Twenty-first century I had come to reject modernism yet needed to re-invent my own artistic stance and this swim was an attempt at that: a rite of passage aiming to retrieve some mode of the classical fused with romantic sensibility. It would not have been possible without Aydogan and Zafir and my sense of victory would not have been so substantial without sharing those few most amicable hours together in that small old *caique*.

However I contemplated these events my feelings had been those of great joy, regardless of how I viewed and reviewed them through the varying lens of literacy. If Byron swam for fame then it is perhaps possible to redefine the truth of fame as an expression of how the axis between nature and the amicably human can be reformed. It is a trajectory that is not, after all, an absolute but needs to be claimed by effort and also by submission to the traditions which enclose such an event. Personally, this occurred through the iteration and practice of poetry and the amiably mimetic endeavour which preceded it.

~ On Friendship ~

II ~ I

HYDRA Island during the latter half of the Twentieth century was one of those unique locations in the history of artistic achievement, for like Paris in the Twenties, or London's Soho during the Thirties, or New York in the Fifties it was a remarkable venue for bohemian life and creativity. There is an exception though, qualifying this comparison, for unlike those cities the community of Hydra was tiny: between two and three thousand inhabitants lived in one small town upon an island that was essentially devoid not only of other human society but also of trees, ground water, and animal life. Hydra is essentially formed of dry sterile rock with some diminutive pine woods and the occasional passage bird; what human society there is occurs within a single settlement that surrounds a port on three sides like a classical theatre. When speaking of Hydra that is what one refers to, this isolated littoral community and not the barren isle.

Hydra remains today an isle without roads and where few ever depart from the town to venture into the hills or to wander toward the coast on the south side. On that other and unpopulated shore there is an older and more pastoral world of the eastern Mediterranean, with smoothly paved threshing circles beside former terraced fields, little one-roomed shepherd dwellings with their cisterns and thorny goat pens, and a *flora* of prickly pear and sage, of wild fig and olive, and arbutus. A few antique signaling stations from centuries ago still remain on hill-tops looking out southwards across a vacant and glittering Aegean.

Architecturally, the buildings of Hydra town arise from another era where

Eighteenth century stone structures define every point of view with radical and finely linear proportion; the grey of rendered mineral moderated by a cerulean sky and immediate azure sea as the stone streets climb upward from the shore. Stark whitewashed walls and paths sharpen one's visual perspective especially during glaring summer months and these strongly optical qualities are visually pleasing in their influence for they have arisen naturally without plan, architectural foresight, or imposition. The audible quietness of the isle, untroubled by motor traffic and due to the geographical remoteness of the community—so separate from the rest of the world—all facilitate an outstanding physical environment, one which began to attract an uncommon group of amicable foreigners in the mid-Twentieth century.

By the Nineteen-Fifties all these exceptional qualities prompted a sudden florescence of cultural achievement in painting, poetry, prose, music, and sculpture, as the isle became the destination and home to both Greek and foreign artists. It was painting however, which became Hydra's most favoured, prolific, and advanced medium.

These lines are written to discover not simply some of the names and substance of those myriad individuals who lived and worked among the Hydriot community during this half-century of years but also to tell of how some of these characters came to succeed in their novel perception and demonstration of 'the beautiful': *to kalo*. Why was it that this geographically removed community became so appealing to a transient group of thoroughly eclectic and sundry outsiders who possessed little historical affinity with each other but who together came to compose a miniature society that was internally sympathetic in so many way? I would submit that this conceptual and emotional coherence was due to the community being intimately founded upon the practice of remarkable friendships and a shared aesthetic aspiration.

It was not so much the natural aspects of life on this isle which attracted and inspired artists but it was more the unique, incomparable, and inimitably enlightening qualities of the society which enticed the painters, poets, musicians, and novelists to this especial situation. There had long been an indigenous tradition of painting and literature on the island, particularly concerning marine depiction, for much of the early wealth of Hydra came from shipping and an economy of nautical commerce. Yet the painters who congregated about the port in the last sixty years were among some of the most innovative and inventive artists of their generation.

Early traditions of painting on Hydra were concerned with the portrayal of sailing vessels and the portraiture of captains and ship-owners and also with representations of heroes of the early Nineteenth century and its War of Independence. It was Nikos Hadji-Kyriakos Gikas who truly conceived and delineated a modernist tradition of landscape art however, one that has continued into the early present century with the pictures of Dimitri Gassoumis, Panagiotis Tetsis, Panagiotis Rappas, Angelika Lialios, and also in the canvases of the Canadian Adam Shapiro. The rare and masterly pastel drawings of Marios Loizides marked the high moment in this pictorial tradition, although these works are difficult to locate nowadays having all entered into the veiled rooms of private collections.

It was during the harsh postwar Fifties that numerous Western painters began to take up residence on *The Rock*, as it was often affectionately titled. Then, the suave Gikas, perhaps the most significant Greek painter of that century, lived and worked from his studio in an old family mansion—now presently a despoiled ruin—above the fishing hamlet of Kamini; many others were attracted by his pioneering visual influence into that circle. The splendid and ancient Gikas domain was home or host to innumerable other artists whom he had befriended or who had sought him out, most notably the painter John Craxton and the eminent *memoirist* Patrick Leigh-Fermor who composed his most well known book *Mani* within those walls. There was a supreme amity and a sharing of means in those days and a similar impassioned admiration for an older, pre-Independence Greece with its late Byzantine and post-Ottoman graphic fashions.

The paintings of that time can be separated into two general divisions: those that depicted terrain and portrayed individuals, and those that tended toward a more ideal formality of abstraction. I am perpetually amazed and nonplussed by how varying are the multitude of perceptions which human beings have access to when they look upon the world, for there is no single optical reality and the manifold distinctions between abstraction and representation and, as a corollary, the differing influences of Western Europe and North American painting genres, played themselves out among these artists. Expressionism, in both its European and American styles, became a powerful presence in the School of Hydra, beginning with the drawings of Brenda Chamberlain and climaxing in the powerful and magnificent work of Brice and Helen Marden.

It was the towering presence of Gikas, who—having lived and studied for many years in Paris where he had been a friend of Le Corbusier—brought the *genus* of cubism to Hydra painting, viewing the town and its vegetation through such a conceptual lens. This was a style that John Craxton carefully developed before he moved away and took up residence on Crete. Then, within this vein of abstract representation came a group of London painters who drew with them the currency of bohemian Soho, Anthony Kingsmill being one of the first of this *coterie* to take up residence on the island in the early Sixties. His work was primarily concerned with the human figure in a manner of expressionist and almost *impasto* abstraction. The younger Kingsmill had been deeply influenced by the English painter Keith Vaughan as well as by the Greek Ioannis Tsarouxis and that abstracted and at times impressionist manner of portraying human form became the mature style of Kingsmill. He also—earlier on—painted island landscapes in the non-figurative mode of the English John Piper. The work of the youthful Guy Allain, a friend of Kingsmill, pursued an extreme expressionism, but his canvases are extremely scarce items today.

The early Gikas style of topographic figuration was magnified by other foreigners on the isle during the latter Twentieth century, by semi-realistic painters like the Canadian Marcella Maltais and presently by Panagiotis Rappas, the descendent of a native painter. The Scottish Jane Porter, whose depictions of views about the town captured the complexity of island architecture and its pictorial planes and transitory guests, moved her model closer towards natural and lyrical illustration. All this pursuit of representation and non-representation culminated in the work of William Pownall—presently a resident of the island for more than fifty years—who developed his field of view into one of almost pure abstraction. Working from a British tradition directed by painters such as Lanyon, Pasmore, and Heron, Pownall has become the paramount non-figurative artist of the isle and his development of a refined minimalism has depicted both images of terrain and of the marine tradition of Hydriot culture. Today Pownall has become an elder statesman of resident foreigners on Hydra.

It is the works of Gikas, of Loizides, and of Marden however, which presently stand at the international apex of such painterly production—particularly in terms of price—yet their canvases were generated within a context of hundreds of other works which, although not commercially so successful nor so aesthetically immaculate and perfect, were nevertheless magnificent in their small capturings of humanistic and earthly views of the insular dimensions of human existence: the physical, emotional, historical, and the ontological dimensions of kinship and affinity. All of these painters existed and worked within an amicable and profoundly egalitarian community where other media—like poetry, prose, music, and sculpture—similarly thrived: this was their larger and most valuable context.

The Greek literary *renaissance* of the first half of the Twentieth century conduced to an early artistic presence on Hydra, with poets like George Seferis and his Athenian cohort frequently visiting the place; one of the *cantos* in his masterpiece *Mythistorema*, poem number Thirteen, is about the naval port of Hydra. Then later, among the literate rather than the painterly—nominally led by the globally famous and now cosmopolitan lyricist Leonard Cohen—were Richard Vick and Piers Kemp, plus innumerable other poets who passed about the community during those years, like the charismatic mariner George Dillon Slater and the ardent neo-Romantic Maria Servaki. The Byronic Vick and his partner, the painter Jane Motley—who was both an impressionist and portraitist—became renowned for their exotic and oriental style of living where the practice of art merged with the being of life itself. Their household and their yacht—both full of painting, sculpture, and the sound of poetry and music—became a refuge for many young artists and performers. Their hospitality and generosity were famed and Vick and Motley became an icon of bohemian style, merging creativity with idealism and a mildly libertine sensibility.

Even among those who were not fine artists in a professional sense there was frequently a passion for exquisite arrangement in terms of domestic living; aesthetes like Lindsey Callicoatt made apparent the immaculate in terms of interior design where rooms and courtyards became sophisticated articulations of a reserved plan of beauty. *Cuisine* became refined and esoteric, gardens were sites of treasured cultivation, and the writing of letters in a world that was pre-digital and where the *Poste Restante* received the mails irregularly—depending upon the weather and sailing conditions for the ferries—was a minor art in itself. All these multi-dimensional practices became extra yet integral components of diurnal and seasonal time among foreign residents, as their world became an exclusive *ethos* in itself. This was a culture of friends, not of fungible economy nor of physiological kinship.

Simultaneously, life for this alien population assumed a performative and expressive quality and it was not simply the making of works of art and the detail of general livelihood which informed the days but also a manner of visible performance, in both fashion and speech, which charged the code of the place. This was a site of unspoken theatre, both physically, given the terrain, and culturally, given the persons involved, and underlying all this was the work of artistry itself, the fuel and consequence of such animated existence. That necessary performative aspect of life became unbearable for some, like the modest John Craxton who fled towards Xania in Crete; others departed for Nauplion or to Lakonia.

Novelists like Felix Thoresen were part of a Norwegian group of artists who arrived on the island in the Sixties and Seventies. There were also sculptors and musicians who spent time on the isle before moving elsewhere: like Palmer, who carved island stone, and Julius White the London sculptor who stayed on Hydra during the latter Seventies, and Paul Thorneycroft who worked in several plastic media. Bjørn Saastad, the painter and photographer, recorded many of his individual friends during these decades, particularly among those who gravitated towards the imaginative household of Timothy Hennessy and Ioannis Kardamatis. There were also the film-makers Ina Fritsche and Nick Broomfield, and the latter's cinematic documentary of those years and characters is soon to be released. Terry Oldfield, the composer and mantic flautist, was a strong presence during the Eighties and played in many venues including the legendary Bill's Bar, itself the arch-stage of performative gesture and choral repetition.

It was these dramatic qualities of life on the island which so propelled the days there with a peripheral yet unspeakable energy. It was this intensely ephemeral yet demonstrative practice of life, especially as it occurred on the port itself, which enclosed that *other* production which happened in the studios or at the desks. Architectonically, the port, being in the shape of a broad amphitheatre—a *scene* that was enveloped on three rising and circular sides by whitened houses and lanes—was exploited by many movie directors who took advantage of this natural set, with Sophia Loren, Merlina Merkouri, Anthony Perkins, and dozens of other stars acting their parts.

One might assert that genius occurs as a symptom of a psyche which is solely able to drive a medium of expression; genius in this sense being a condition of activity rather than an inherent or material quality of human consciousness. Yet as with the poor and gossiping women of the Theban royal family in the *Bakxai* of Euripides, the release or amplification of such symptoms can cause marvellous delusion and automatic death; for to be able to call upon one's psychic silhouette and to control that mental and emotional verve—which are usually suppressed and socially or personally ordered—requires extreme tenacity and resolute habituation. This is what we think of as nowadays as genius, that intensely precise focus or indestructible aim which is only true. Many succumbed to such personal phrasing, both privately or publically, and yet from this ingenious impalpable theatre arose an abundant number of works of great loveliness and superlative registry.

In one of his last books, *Civilisation And Its Discontent*, published in Nineteen-Thirty, Sigmund Freud spoke about the cultural unease and disquiet caused when society becomes overly complicated as it simultaneously denies its own store of generative agency, until, at some tensile instant there is a sudden exfoliation of this invisible vigour which pitilessly deforms and deranges the deficient world of conventional illusion. It was this tactful balance however, this equilibrium of public manner and personal emotion, coupled with the discipline and strength of effort, which enabled most of these successful painters and writers to secure fulfillment. On the one hand there was an indiscriminate use of alcohol and narcotics and yet, on the other hand, wonderful objects of luminous beauty were brought to light. These were not only painting but also poetry, song, and sculpture, born into a realm of humanity and yet with the impartial air of the casual and informal. All this was driven by a determination to exceed anything temporal or mortal and to go beyond the constraint of typical and habitual perception and towards a condition of the completely affirmative.

Some, like myself for instance, found solace and equipoise on the other—the southern—side of the island where no one lived and where there were only a few rough paths, cisterns, and here and there occasional shallow terraces for the cultivation of barley. Much poetry was to be found among those desiccated hills and along that unpeopled coast of grey rock, thyme, and a few hawks, such was its ancient and natural harmony; it was on that farther and other shore of Hydra that happiness and a certain symmetry of life was available for those who were able to put aside the performative and hyper-productive world of the port and find a pacific retreat amongst the silence of a more telluric and marine world.

This community persisted for just over fifty years and still nowadays continues to flourish but in a completely altered and more level manner, with resident painters like the Franco-Australian Jill Appert and the English Pauline Keaney; Hydra has become European and put aside its Levantine dress. That prior society had been primarily established upon a profound relationship with the Hydriot people who completely embraced all these strange and unconventional artists and accepted them into their own anciently traditional and originally Albanian community regardless of the occasional extreme and compulsively non-orthodox antics. Without the Hydriots none of this life or aesthetic culture would have been possible for the friendships which enabled and drove the foreign community were inherently grounded upon a far more intrinsic degree of amity and community with the islanders themselves. Without the local Greeks who supported all this sometimes uncanny and *sauvage* enterprise this artistic venture could not have been in any way viable.

Perhaps the most dynamic social quality of this period was what could be described as utopian and I would aver that this social pattern derives from an earlier and deeply traditional Greek or Middle Eastern ethic of hospitality. It was not simply the case that an *ethnos* of tremendous and lively creativity was at work on the isle nor that this community of artists was unlike other communities due to the geographical isolation, the natural confinement of the town and port, and to its mutual aesthetic ideals: this sharing of livelihood and aspiration, of ideals and of actual *praxis* was—I would argue—matchless, and was in fact utopian. Not only were ideas and conversations exchanged but also houses, material sustenance, tools like tubes of pigment, typewriters, paper, canvas, books, and other artists' materials, as well as—for the purposes of a visa during the years of dictatorship—hard-currency banknotes.

The coherent society which obtained among these foreigners was directed at producing works of art in various media yet there existed a simultaneous and mutual condition of support for this which was not simply amicable and familiar but also economic. It was this aspect of the foreign community which made it exceptional and so unlike other such European societies during the modern period. The means of production were shared and exchanged just as were the ideas and visible extensions, for co-operation was the medium rather than competition. Yet this collaboration was founded upon one's ability to sustain extremes of experience and of intoxication and, at some point, upon the validity or necessity of speech acts, which came into play and justified the certainty of one's *agonistic* identity.

So this is what happens when a culturally diverse group of young and alien people are assembled in one small location that is benignly separated from the rest of life, by the sea and by the fact that a boat only visits perhaps once a day if the weather is good. This is what happens when these persons do not really need to labour and work in order to live and survive whilst they are in pursuit of aesthetic experience and there are no social nor even moral constraints upon their daily activity and personal sympathies.

Such ambition for what might be construed as artistic truth was one that was concomitant with a freedom from inhibition and responsibility and borne within such gorgeous terrain and topography as well as being encompassed by a coruscating and vivid marine world. All this combined to effect a superb super-creativity, yet without discipline and mental restraint this was often simply a direct route towards affective suffering and *pathos*. Nevertheless there occurred the production of magnificent works of art, as evinced by an exhibition which is to be staged in Athens during the summer of Two Thousand and Nineteen.

I would assert that this is the almost Dionysian mystery of human creativity, here made effective insofar as the scene was limited to one solitary location upon an isolated rocky extrusion of a desolate and steep fifty square kilometres. This was the pragmatic criterion that was perhaps the governing metaphor for life on Hydra, for such creativity is actually the hard white core that underlies all human association and affection.

An event of this nature is rare in human experience and time if not unique. One thinks of Fifth century Athens, or of *renaissance* Florence, or of Mathura in India in the mid-First Millennium B.C.E. There are many such locations in cultural history of intense universal fusion where objects of severe aesthetic beauty were fabricated; yet the isolation of Hydra as an island and the distinction of the town and its port made this moment and these individuals most uncommon and, in retrospect, often distinguished.

Needless to say there were suicides and young deaths and the incidence of extensive drug use and a passionate consumption of alcohol led to much *malaise*, often with long-term and generational defection: for not only did the parents often die or suffer from mental instability but so too did their offspring. There was a strange admixture of extra-ordinary inspiration and ingenuity with what can be termed a corollary of self-destructiveness: for those who did not succeed in sustaining their vision of absolute beauty might be consumed in that effort or became thoroughly enervated by the process.

All communities own patterns of kinship, how it is that men and women join and regenerate and how it is that sexual unions are agreeably arranged. On Hydra during this period of the late Twentieth century—during the post-war epoch that focussed about the Sixties with its habits of carnal promiscuity and mobility—sensual congress was various and diverse and genuinely transient. Few marriages were celebrated and yet children were born. In a sense it was the intimacy of the work and of the engaged artistry which took priority over any emotional affect of kin. Sorrow and jealousy existed yet there was equally a communal and *idiorhythmic* vision, an undertaking which superceded all else. It was the work and not the life which became the ultimate criterion and yet paradoxically it was a collective of friendship which sustained this. Even the dreadful ordeals wreaked by the onset of the HIV epidemic in the Nineties were survived, although not by everyone.

Such practices of course were neither original nor innovative; there had been the bohemia of Soho in London at turn of the last century, or the mid-century Beat culture of New York and California, and the *nouvelle vague* of Paris. The Twenties in London, Paris, and Berlin were of a similar nature for artists who developed the neo-Romantic antinomian manners of the previous century, where radicals and travellers typified by the genre of Wordsworth, Shelley, or Turner, flourished so victoriously. What happened on Hydra though was concentrated into a small extent of earthly and stony terrain and consequently, the emotions and passions were likewise condensed and compressed, particularly in terms of human amity but also in terms of an appreciation of natural, terrestrial, architectural, and marine beauty. Hence a new species of Philhellenism evolved in this rare locale.

Yet none of this community of artists would have been possible without the benign alliance of the Hydriot people; just as at times the Immortals are said to descend upon the earth and to walk upon the ground, to dine and to converse with humankind and sometimes to make love with them, perhaps occasionally imparting some of their divine cognisance and foresight during those moments of reserved and intimate encounter.

A few of the older generation of Hydriots are still with me in my mind's eye and heart's cell; they were the *autochthons*, those who arose from the earth itself and whose lives were born from many generations of Hydriot marriages and households. There was Maria Goulas who ran a little shop high up on the hill in the Kiafa district; her family also looked after the church next to the store. She belonged to that old and faithful world of Orthodoxy, a generation who had known of the Dictator Metaxas and the ensuing Nazi Occupation and then, of the Civil War and the subsequent horribly cruel conflict between Communists and the Nationalists; she also, like so many, lived through the crude dictatorship of the Colonels. All that experience was visible in her features, so much suffering and yet such gentle fortitude and sure reverence. I well recall the afternoon when her son-in-law was found hanging from the balcony to their house and how Maria endured even that grief. Since the days of Andromakhe and of Briseis, lament has always been an inherent part of Greek musical *genre*; and in that view what we have lost and forsaken is eternally more beautiful than what we might ever possess. That grief remains like the shadow of a fish in water, yet it is always to be conveyed.

There was also Kyria Sophia who was aged, faithful, and lived above her *taverna* which was on the way up the hill towards Kala Pigadia; she sold wine and sometimes continued to entertain, at Easter especially. She lived in great pain from her legs and her later years were an ordeal; she was one of the last of the Hydra women to wear a head-scarf. There was also old Maria—the only woman muleteer on the isle—who lived beside the inland and paved path towards Kamini; she was unmarried and she too was one of the few to still wear the head-scarf. Her house was next door to the candle-maker who could be seen in those years pouring redolent bees-wax onto suspended threads. Maria's mother must have had some terrible condition like syphilis for she often sat upon the marble threshold blankly looking out upon the world as it passed along the path, her face terribly scarred and wounded.

There was Ioannis Kremos whose family had the last ships' chandlery down on the port, dating back to the century before when stone quais had not been built and vessels were simply drawn up onto the sandy shore; he also lived above his shop but had a country house out beyond Vlyko to the south. In the Seventies, chandlery had given way to tourist items and that kind of quick commerce as the old and new worlds exchanged, the Levantine becoming European. In his youth Ioannis had been at sea, like most of the male Hydriots, and he loved to tell stories about brothels and prostitutes which he would illustrate with pencil drawings upon the shop's soft grey wrapping paper.

There was also Gregorios who was a gardener who carved figures in the wood which he brought home from his prunings. My wife and I still have a group of four heads as well as many wooden spoons that he once fashioned. Like most of his kind, Gregori's marriage had been arranged and his bride had come to the island from a small village to the south on mainland Peloponnisos; I actually know that Lakonian village well. The ground floor of his Hydra house was empty except for a gigantic loom at which his three or four daughters were always working. Theirs was one of the happiest families that I knew on the isle, always lightly replete with goodness, lucid kindness, and easy endeavour.

It makes me sad to think that these people—and they are but a few of many—are no longer in the world and that their Greece too has vanished along with its virtuous generosity and dignified human compassion. Their undeviating and candid goodwill towards the foreigners on the isle was unconditioned and without expectation and they extended their empathy and benevolence with such open propriety: friendship being an obligation and hospitality always a necessity to those who entered their community. This was a rule.

The modern philhellenes are now the young middle class Greeks themselves who attempt to revision and reconstruct a former pre-modern livelihood, a lost nature which has been so submerged by Europe. I always feel slightly melancholic now when I return to Hydra, for it is as if one does not actually exist any more, being unrecognised and unseen, which is a strangely transparent condition and not mortal. That former decency and generosity that was always without judgment no longer supplies the social currency with its tokens.

It is not simply that an economy—when ploughing was done with a yoke of mules, when harvests were taken in with sickles, and the threshing and the winnowing that ensued were accomplished with rites of joy, or when in windy October the winy *musto* arrived aboard *caiques* and the port was noisy with a tap-tapping of coopers as they caulked their barrels with dry palm frond and rinsed the stale lees from the containers with sea-water—but that a most ancient sensibility for the natural and sentient *tempo* of this earth has been harshly forsaken. Open friendship was a convention intrinsic to that world and a mark of dignity.

It is as if a steel blade of technology has severed the knowledge, awareness, and traditions of what must amount to several thousand years of human experience and that these have been suddenly put away and forgotten. Maria Goulas, Kyria Sophia and their kind of humanity are no more, and that imagery of life—once so well recorded through the lens of Fred Boissonnas, an hundred years ago—has perished.

So, imagine that if you were present at a future exhibition of the work of some of these artists, it would actually be a virtual representation of the island and its foreign public and that those pictures, drawings, and photographs, presented a totality of visual field: the buildings, seascapes, the landscape, as well as images of the *personae* involved in those years, and also and most importantly, their inner and conceptual belief in human, moral, and sometimes transcendental life. Imagine too that you could hear the declamation of their poetry and prosaic speech, their stringed and woodwind music, and could appreciate the fabulous benificence and utopian kindness of life then, amongst the foreigners and between the Hydriots and the rest of island society. Despite the madness, the unbearable addictions, the sexual desperation, and the drive of relentless ambition, this small brief world of Hydra during the latter half of the Twentieth century would be recollected, barely captured and re-enacted in the paintings and images that would be momentarily staged in a hall of two-dimensional planes by such a show.

What was a profoundly formative few seconds in the history of Western art would be suddenly presented to you in a temporary and transitive remodelling which reforms and so recollects that passing narrative and offers you a narrow view of its aesthetic, ethical, and visionary life. This was a world come of human trial and industry and sustained by the emotion and affects of passion and remorse; yet, as you would see, the sum of so much endeavour and revelation was unique and far more than a mere sum of its multitude of parts. This was an invisible place reified, realised, and made complete by inspiration and profoundly shared experience: particularly in the acute and oblique perceptions of Gikas, the long and agile view of Brice Marden, the terrific yet silent *kosmos* of Marios Loizides, and the subtly reductive mind of Pownall.

The remarkable assembly of this group of completely assorted people who—before their arrival on the isle had little previous intimacy and certainly no genetic contact—have produced one of the notable moments in Western art history. For a brief while there was in this small theatre of the creative and performative an uncommon and unorthodox society based solely upon friendship, acquaintance, and occasionally love, and supercharged with a mutual pursuit for the perfection of artistic ideal and truth. These miscellaneous and highly various individuals inhabited the terrestrial cauldron of the port and its immediate topography and actually made their well-tempered works into something tangible and durable, many items of which are now held as fine and coveted masterpieces in museums.

Even the uninhibited *hetairai* and *hetairoi* who remain undetected today, who simply drank and smoked, danced and sunbathed, made love and perhaps read novels, even they were a vivid and intrinsic part of the community, and their freedom of living and of corporeal expression were a crucial aspect in the unlimiting and enhancing of the other lives in that civil group, the ones actively engaged in artistic production. In the Platonic *Phaido*, in the dream that came to Sokrates, the voice tells him, *Mousiken poiei kai ergazou*, 'make poetry and make it work'. The painters and the poets, musicians, novelist, sculptors, photographers, film-makers, who made this music on late Twentieth century Hydra, were extremely motive and modern, but it was the others, the lovers and the companions, the friends, who, listening to that invisible heart's clear bell, truly made it work.

The retrospective exhibition that is soon to be held in Athens records some of those moral and mental exertions and their inspired instants where the beautiful became briefly received and apparent, to be tentatively yet precisely imitated in one material form or another. Today on the island there are a number of private collections of works generated during that half century of intense and amplified production and the coming exhibition shall stand witness to the perspicacity, generosity, and the intellectual clarity of those early patrons and collectors, for they too were a singularly vibrant component of that brief association among friends.

~ On Friendship ~

II ~ II

EARLY one June morning I slipped an old red bag over my shoulders, locked the door, and putting the key under a rock on the window sill, paused for a moment to feel grateful to the house where I had been staying. I took my stick and set off across the dust on a walk. The Greek sun had not long been up and the air still retained some of the freshness of night and soon I had trodden down the waterless stream bed, a path of flat grey stones that squeaked and grated with dryness, had passed the agave, a plant that only rises and blooms every seven years—this one, during the last month, had shot up to well over twenty feet—and reached the thin road that ran along the edge of the sea. There I turned southward and then began to ascend into the tawny leonine hills of the Peloponnese.

I had walked in many places, Scotland, northern Spain, France, Rwanda, and Saurasthra, but this time I knew that I was setting out on something more special and purposeless: this time I had nowhere to go and for once, no constraints of time. I was heading south down towards the peninsula of Cape Maleas, what in the antiquity of Pausanias—a Second century travel writer and also a walker—had been known as Bion, a region in the lowest reaches of the province of Sparta. Maleas was the most orient of the three promontories that ran out towards Africa.

Now, several decades later, as I sit at my desk on a third floor in Cambridge—just as the dawn comes and a cold north wind is rattling the windows and playing with the young daffodils in the garden below, as the crews set out on the river in their eights beginning to prepare for another season on the water, and as the steam gurgles and hisses through the radiators—I sit here amidst heavy Sanskrit quartos and notebooks trying to reconstruct the dimensions of that walk and its meaning. For in a sense, the walk continued until last summer—it was a very long walk indeed, in my heart and mind—when I returned to Maleas with three friends. Then, on foot, we descended to a disused lighthouse at the most south-eastern tip of Europe.

Walking for me has always been, at its best, a contemplative action, a slowing down of process and a tranquillising of perception. One proceeds across a landscape with a sense of objective disclosure as place reveals itself and becomes a companion and makes itself more apparent as a slow terrestrial intimacy is established. To walk is ideally to be self-effacing, one moves out of time as we are transformed by the distance, and if the walk is good we transcend both personal situation and terrain.

I had been staying in that small four-square house by the sea since the previous summer; the name of the place was Limonas and it had been lent to me by a wonderful English friend. In return, before I left I whitewashed all the walls and cut sufficient bamboo from a stand beside the stream-bed to roof over a trellis which shaded the terrace and supported two vines. It was a handsome house then and extremely simple; it had a sandy floor and bamboo ceilings and a red tiled roof and stood close to the sea at the bottom of a long valley of olive and citrus; it was the only dwelling in the area. There was a deep well at the back of the house from where I took my water and washed. Every ten days or so I used to walk the coast road into town, about eleven kilometres away, to purchase bread and tea and a few other stores and to visit the post office. The serene solitude and tranquillity of Limonas was such that I always felt strange walking into Monembasia and meeting people or talking with the farmers who would occasionally give me a lift was always an eerie experience. I used to feel that I was coming from nowhere and had to work hard to recall my social self.

During the previous year, my wife—together with our small son—had been living in a hamlet to the north called Richea. I used to sometimes walk up there to visit them and stay a few days before returning to the coast. That had been an eight or nine hour walk which skirted the edge of the sea before turning inland into a wonderful and enchanting vale full of some of the most ancient olive groves I have ever seen: huge squat trees gnarled and hollowed by centuries of cultivation. Once Monembasia had been passed and one had reached the shore just to its north, that landscape became breathtaking and even now I remain fascinated by those memories and images.

After Monembasia, for almost an hour the path towards Richea ran along a yellow beach with steep silvery cliffs behind it—typical of the Lakonic coast—before it turned inland, away from any sign of habitation; the massive rock of Monembasia vanished and there was only land, sea, and stone and a few rough olive or fig trees. One passed an old Byzantine signalling station out upon a promontory with a tiny bay beneath it where fishing boats would sometimes anchor during the day before setting off to haul or drop nets at twilight. There was one isolated cistern on that track where I used to drink, otherwise there were only figs or the occasional wild pear tree with which to allay thirst.

The way continued north for many kilometres before reaching the port of Zarax whose unique geological formation—for Greece—was in the shape of a small *fjord*. Above it the cyclopean walls of an archaic citadel stood, immobile and perfectly assembled. That walk contained some of the most joyous hours of my life, because of its views, its tranquillity, and its spirit of place which I never encountered elsewhere. It had a wildness that recalled the west of Scotland—there was a similar lyricism about the scene—and the stones of Zarax captured me like no other site has ever done. Even today I have a picture of three of those giant, perfectly mortised, ravishingly grey rocks, here beside my desk.

In the spring of that year, when we had first moved down to Lakonia from the island of Hydra, I had stayed with my wife up in the village of Richea, and each afternoon with our son in a rucksack on my back we had explored and roamed those hills and paths. We must have walked a thousand kilometres together across that wild topography discovering every tree and ruin and every bay, every isolated chapel.

There were two particularly unusual features to the region: one, was the phenomenon of upright and wind-eroded rock formations, something that I had only ever seen in Tanzania: *kopjes*, I think they were called, and they were a formation much favoured by leopards. Ironically, the first time that we had ever visited Zarax and had been making a descent of the valley—it was in the depths of winter and our son was still a small baby—I had remarked upon this geological formation and mentioned Africa. When we reached the bay of Zarax later on that day there were some Africans working on an extension to the quai. I spoke with some of them in the evening, enquiring as to what brought them there. They were sailors, presently without a berth, and had been recruited in the Piraeus as labour; their home was in Dar-es-Salaam.

The other unusual feature was the presence of oak trees, something that was unique, in my eyes, to the Peloponnese; perhaps up in Arcadia there were oaks, but they were extremely rare in the south. The acorns displayed a fine foliation of little spikes so that they appeared to be stiff yellowish-green flowers. They were rare, beautiful, and decidedly patrician trees.

As my son and I roamed during those afternoons he would often fall asleep and would stop talking and there would just be the squeak of canvas upon aluminium frame, the quiet sound of my steps over the hot dusty ground, the knock of a pebble now and then, and the tap of my stick.

The cane of a walker is a crucial item in his or her paraphernalia. It is the primary companion, intimate with its grain and knots and balance, and if the walker is not on the flat it is a vital component of equilibrium providing an extra element of extensive stability, something that is extremely important on irregular paths. My particular stick came from Mount Athos, a region that I had walked with a composer friend one Christmas many years before; in fact it was not long after I had just met my wife-to-be and immediately before I visited Cambridge for the first time.

~ On Friendship ~

As good pilgrims—and for pilgrims or *saunterers*, walking is ideally a rite in which physical trajectory modifies their personal being in life—as good pilgrims we had circumambulated the Holy Mountain. It had been wintry and cold and the skies were at times inclement but it had been a stunning walk, one of the best, and we returned back from that ecclesiastical geography to Thessaloniki and then Athens dazed by the vigour and sublimity of the experience. I had flown off towards Boston leaving behind those lovely old deserted monasteries and their many abandoned hermitages. My cane came from there, was tall and made of smooth pale oak in the shape of a Greek *taph*. It was the kind of stick that rhapsodes held when declaiming their verse in classical times, as illustrated on black and red-figure vases.

As I set out that June morning my mood was both low and elated. It was a struggle to leave the lovely little house with its solitude and harmony. On one of the roof posts of the terrace was a dried wreath of poppy and marigold brought to me by a friend on May the first. She was the *fiancée* of a local fisherman who lived in the next bay and she often used to visit to talk about literature; sometimes, if I was out walking, she would leave on my table fossilised shells which she had gathered from nearby cliffs. An elderly farmer, who had some land in the valley behind the house, also visited now and then. He used to bring tomatoes or occasionally some bread that his wife had baked and we used to sit and tell stories, or he would recount to me the news which he had heard on the radio. Those two companions were my only interlocutors whilst living on that shore.

I had done a lot of work in that house, some of it later published in a book called *Eros*. It was as if all the effort of the previous years—first living on the isle of Paros where Archilokhos the proto-poet of Greek lyric had been, and then on Hydra—it was as if all those years of diligence had just been a preparation for what I wrote at Limonas, a prelude as it were. Thus I felt a pang of remorse as I set out that morning in the cool air, the sun still low and rufous upon the horizon and the cicadas not yet aroused to their intense staccatic frenzy. A hoopoe that lived among the wild pear trees near the stream flew about me momentarily.

The tract between Zarax and Maleas, and in particular the region just south of Monembasia, was a *locale* that I had come to love deeply; and for me, place is as significant in life as person. Then, setting out and going away, up over the ridge and putting it all behind, was distressing. There was something timelessly grand about those hills and declivities, their antique groves, the old Ottoman farms, the Byzantine and Venetian influence of Monembasia itself with its unique architecture and fortifications: I had grown to love all that with a sense of profound immediacy which had come from walking its paths and roads.

Also, that particular area, for a couple of miles, was unlike the rest of the coast, insofar as there was a gentleness to the slope of terrain unlike the stark abruptness of most of the region. The landscape was pink and leonine in colour, silvered by expanses of olive, which when the wind blew strongly tossed and foamed like a sea. It was an area that reminded me strongly of East Africa—which to me is one of the most magnificent places on earth—and it also reminded me of the part of southern China where I had been born and lived as a child. There was a complex and wonderful familiarity about that landscape of Limonas and as I set off in the dawn I felt that something untroubled and chaste was slipping away from my life: not so much as a place but as a vision or condition, an emotion. It was as if I were irreversibly forsaking an old friend.

Whilst I was resident in that house, each afternoon during the autumn and then the winter months, after I had finished working I would set off in one direction or another to walk and empty my activated mind. I had two small tortoise-shell cats, neither of which had names, and often they used to accompany me for a while before turning back to the house. Sometimes I would go inland, behind the building, up through the groves into the hills to where a few old Turkish farms lay in states of collapse. There were also some devastated chapels up there overgrown with brambles and genista. The farms had extensive irrigation systems, cisterns and channels, and the fallen buildings manifest an easy grandeur about their presence, with carved stone lintels to the windows and doors and barrel-vaulted ceilings to the lower rooms. At one particular establishment the lemon trees had run wild and had grown into a huge and twisted forest, their bark black with time and the leaves thick and coarsely viridian.

At other times I would head south, along a narrow zinc-coloured coastal track, down towards the headlands which jutted out from the mountainous spine all the way towards Maleas, strangely distant and luminous and immaterial as it hovered in the light above a molten sea. Eagles and hawks would be circulating on the air currents, whistling and mewing, and sometimes I would hear fox cubs barking, to be muted by their mother as I approached. No one was down there except for an occasional farmer pruning his olives or inspecting his holding. In the months before spring came, the hills were often empurpled with flowering heather or sage blooming in delicate mauve petals. I used to know exactly where the most anemones grew or where there were banks of cyclamen, especially the unusual white ones, or where to find the modest prussian-blue orchids. I had also come across a small chapel which still retained its old frescoed walls, although certain of the figures, saints and martyrs, had been defaced and their eyes disfigured.

Sometimes I would visit particular hill tops, other times certain groves, one fig plantation I often went to for it was so ideally situated and mature; I would lie down on that steep slope and watch the sea and the clouds passing above the marine waters. Then I would return home as evening fell and the first bats began to pierce the air and a vixen would cough and if it was dark by the time I arrived at the house perhaps a jackal would slide past in the shadows, giving a horrible shriek as it retreated into the night. An owl always came and sat upon the gables in the early dusk, making a low whoo-whooing call. The two cats would come out to meet me, and occasionally, if I came home before dusk, a ferret would be happily investigating my kitchen or a bird would be flying around inside the rooms and the cats would be pre-occupied. In spring there were a lot of small rose-coloured snakes, slowly and stupidly waking up from their sleep, lying about on stones among the lupins, trying to warm their blood.

I missed my son in those days for he was in Cambridge and I used to write to him of an evening with two lamps flickering on either side of my typewriter. I never ever shut the door of that house unless a storm blew down from the north and churned up the sea: the sound of breakers on the shore boomed ceaselessly for days then and the shutters of the house used to tremble noisily. Salt from the waves covered and bleached everything and the windows were thickly filmed. I always used to turn in early and then rise before the sun except during full moon nights when I would often go walking in the hills; the dense abstract light imparted a metaphysical air to the landscape, illuminating the solitary earth in a lunar monochrome, immersing the world. The cats would often accompany me on those nocturnal walks into the empty powdery hills. Even nowadays, here in the city, if I ever waken before dawn and the moon is shining upon the rooves, I instantly recollect those times, those walks, for their motionless a-temporal clarity in which even the grey silence was suspended.

I had first visited Monembasia on board the Fife ketch *Eilean*, a yacht that I had been navigator and mate of in the Seventies, as it made its way out across the Mediterranean and into Atlantic. We put in late at night and tied alongside the three-masted sailing vessel *Zeus* and then left before morning. All that I recall of the place was the enormous rock of the citadel. The second time that I arrived there was in the early Eighties, when my wife and I had been walking in Lakonia; we were living then on Hydra and had left the isle in the autumn for a week or two of strolling together. We had come down to the coast from inland and had been captivated by the beauty of old Monembasia, for in those days it was much in decay and at that time of the year, deserted and gently melancholic, very much in the romantic tradition. The Morea, which was the mediaeval and Albanian name of the province, became an intrinsic part of our lives, focussing us both in time and place. My wife, who had once practiced as an architect in Paris, designed a house down there for a friend, a dwelling that was to become in many ways our true home and gravity, our concept of what household meant. In those days there were more paths than roads in that region and there were still villages in the hills that were without electricity or public ways.

As I ascended the track towards the ridge that morning, winding back and forth up the steep hill, the countryside lay beneath me lost in blank perspective, with Monembasia in the distance and the headlands up to Zarax beyond. To the south were the promontories before Maleas, hazy and indistinguishable in the nacreous summer light. Out at sea the horizon did not exist as water and sky fused in an increasingly metallic screen, titanic and fierce. One or two minute sails floated in the glare and just off the causeway leading out to Monembasia rock a three-master had anchored in the light.

My old red rucksack sat loosely upon my shoulders—it had been with me for almost two decades of walking on four continents—and my Athos stick was happily balanced in my right hand, resting upon fingertips. As I passed through a village nestled high on the crest where mimosa and walnut trees lined the way, I could hear a young mother with a small boy remarking upon the two loaves that were tied to my bag and the water bottle slung beneath them. "Look at the bread", she said to the child. I had made one monumental error though, something very foolish for a seasoned walker like myself: for I was wearing shorts and a shirt and had the previous week acquired a pair of canvas shoes, the sort of wear that I preferred. Absent-mindedly I had not worn them before setting off and soon my feet were torn and bleeding.

I paused at the top of the range for one final glance backwards, troubled that it was passing away, for I knew that I would never live there again; one might visit and stay but to live there would be no longer possible, not for many years anyway. Perhaps I might return but the idyll was over, that ageless period of one's youth and its pastoral. What lay ahead was unknown and indiscernible. Small grains of grief were with me that day.
I walked for hours as the sun moved towards its zenith. Briefly, at one chapel, it was possible to view both sides of the peninsula; there, being so high, the air was cool and breezy, in fact the wind was raucous and buffetting and I looked

down upon the backs of four eagles playing in the void. I went into the chapel and lit three candles and rested a while in the cold dark air, so luxurious after the bronze hammers of the light outside. As I descended to the plain below the temperature rose to well over an hundred and the brightness was as if made of iron pounding upon one's forehead.

At one point where I paused before entering onto the plain, I halted beneath a carob tree beside a small spring; water was unusual in that terrain and a source of great pleasure for its refreshment and cool. Some wrens flitted among the bamboos and a long thin blue snake idled across the mottled surface of a pool. Fortuitously, another walker approached and we greeted each other; I offered him some of my biscuits and he sat down; I had seen him several times before in Monembasia but we had never spoken. This was the fellow who was many years later to inherit and own the house that my wife had designed for our friend. We soon parted, he going up the road from where I had come.

I reached the small town of Neapolis—the Naples of the region—by dusk. It was a discreet accumulation of summer houses for Athenians with a row of café terraces stretched along the beach. It took me a while to find a room for the night—the town was so busy—a tiny windowless compartment with an Italian couple beyond a partition who made love for hours. Exhausted, I sank into that gloom and slept naked upon the metal bed, woken periodically by the sounds of frequently mingled passion. My ankles and toes were on fire with acute pain and I was intoxicated by the day's dehydration and effort.

The first three days of an excursion are always an agony, as one's muscles and feet accommodate: shoulders, legs, all the body has to adjust to a *tempo* of ambulation, walking hour after hour. Conditions then were difficult due to the reckless heat and lack of water. I found a pharmacy and bought some zinc tape and plasters and located a quiet café. My only book was a small collected Shakespeare given to me by an American friend one Easter many years before; that morning I read some Lear. I memorised a lot of speeches during the walk, for it lasted well over forty days.

To the south-west lay the island of Kythera, large, opaque, and distant, and the land of Aphrodite; we had been there some years before in January with two companions and their month-old baby. The weather had been tempestuous and no boats had been able to land for weeks and we had been stranded in the port, making forays on foot about the island. To the north-east lay the low spit of Elaphonisos, which is where I next proceeded towards, walking barefoot all morning along the coast with its occasional tamarisk trees and soothing my feet in the sea. A small landing-craft served as a ferry across a shallow aquamarine channel.

The single town on the isle was almost Kykladic in design, totally unlike the architecture of the mainland. Its streets were sandy and each dwelling possessed a walled garden with vines and mulberry trees for shade. I soon found the one baker and took on my usual supply of two loaves and a few packets of tea-biscuits, all that I could carry. My one luxury was a bottle of sweet cold orange soda, which in that temperature provided a pleasure close to ecstasy for my fluid levels were so low. Someone had told me about a beach on the other side of the isle which was pristine and unknown and I soon found the path in that direction and set off. It was dusk again by the time I reached the other side.

The cove was truly gorgeous, almost Caribbean with a great stretch of hot clean sand and nothing but the wreck of an abandoned coaster far up on the shore that appeared ghostly and surreal being completely out of context. One afternoon I hauled myself up its anchor chain to inspect the vessel, but it was spooky and filthy and I abandoned the project. It had been the same when I had dived upon a sunken Italian cruiser off Port Sudan many years before: there is something about wrecked and abandoned ships that is poignant, forlorn, as well as ghastly.

On that first evening I soon discovered a low well inland from the shore and filled my bottle with a stale brackish supply. Up on a rocky headland that protruded from the middle of the beach I settled for the night and for a week that became home. I slept lying upon my sleeping bag, resting my sore feet until I could set out again, slowly allowing my legs and joints to attune to a rhythm of extensive walking.

No other human being was anywhere near that place, it was like a desert, the Sahara on the Red Sea coast, saline and gravelly with a sea intensely salt and turquoise. A scrap of shadow was such a relief from the fury of the sunlight and I spent the hottest hours of the day in the shade of a holm oak. I wore nothing during that time except when I went to the well or when I walked back across the isle into town to buy bread. I used to frequently swim in the hot sea for hours at a time, exploring the western rim of the coast, nothing but black rocks and boiling sand. At night as I lay on my sleeping bag listening to the waves curling softly onto the shore below I could see the lights of ships passing east and west and hear the low thrum of their engines.

Soon the walk began to settle into me and my mood and thoughts moved deeply towards Maleas, the abstract, ontological Maleas of antiquity and idea. Apart from the baker's wife, a slovenly gravid and yet greatly attractive woman, I spoke with no one and only occasionally admitted myself the oblivion of an orange soda. Days and evenings were passed thinking, writing, watching the landscape and sea, and the sky at night with all its vividly inscripted constellations and mobile planets; I had first learned their names and shapes when navigating the *Eilean* across Atlantic. Gradually my walk began to take hold of me as my feet healed and I became more and more joined and engaged with the landscape. By then I had moved on to Romeo and Juliet and thence to Othello: "It is the cause, it is the cause ... let me not name it to you ..."

Originally, paths were made by animals and followed by human beings, human migration and human development were closely involved and arguably remain so nowadays. Walking, along with the construction of tools and the domestication of fire, was one of humanity's earliest gestures towards social affiliation: habitual relations were inspired and acts of repetition assumed plural, agreeable, and sometimes political state. Walking took those early bipedal creatures away from the familiar and led to the population of the entire planet and was the origin of humanity's dissemination upon earth. Similarly, for a nomad, walking approximated to a condition of the hypostatic insofar as it aimed at neither material accumulation nor adherence to objects; perhaps conflict only came with settlement and ideally, today, the art of walking reiterates that wonder of extent. It was such a frame of mind that I began to settle into, with the exception that I was alone with only landscape for companionship.

To go a walk is inadmittedly or not, to refound that pre-historical past that has been profoundly lost from our traditions or has been covered over from sensibility. It is to refind a natural order that is not instituted by any search for knowledge but quite the opposite, it is to restore that pre-social world in which rational conscious does not form a part. This state could be construed as either subliminal or beautiful, frightening or wonderful, in which one transcends the normal and mundane.

In a sense, to go a solitary walk nowadays off into a deserted landscape, reformulates something of that prior condition: there is a movement away from the civil or the settled, away from the domain of human law, towards the wild and uncivilised. Out there is the region of the periphery, the world that is *out*-law, that is, a world of freedom unmediated by human refinement or temper. If we cannot approach or perceive the absolute perhaps at least we can view its margin, that area where categories of human thought cease to apply or occur. Walking as an art attempts to refine that boundary, to recuperate the sensible and insensible.

That marked the beginning of my journey, as I patrolled the far shores of Elaphonisos, letting my feet heal themselves and allowing my psyche to gravitate to this new and undomestic living. Weeks later when I returned to society, those first nights of sleeping in rooms were disconcerting if not mildly horrifying for their hygienic sterility.

Once my blisters had repaired themselves I packed away my sleeping bag and Shakespeare and notebook and moved. By then my body had become dry and dusted with salt and stained by the sunlight. I returned to the village and took the landing-craft back towards the mainland and made my way towards

Neapolis. This time I did not stay in a room but continued past the town, arriving at dusk in a tiny bay. The path that I took was along the edge of the water and the stratification of the rocks there was most uncommon: a deep crimson mineral in fluid layers as if formerly lava. I slept upon those rocks beneath some acacia and a few palms near two small closed-up houses that were set back from the water. When I had been in Neapolis the week before I had purchased a postcard on which two finely proportioned houses with several palm trees were displayed; only now did I realise that this was the *venue* of the picture.

It was at this point that my walk really began to assume its form and to become significant, to possess me, as it were, and I simply accorded with its impetus. I had read the relevant passages in Pausanias and knew how populous this area had been in late classical times yet now it was singularly uninhabited. Before the sun had risen over the ridge next morning I had swum and shaved and was already on the road back into Neapolis. I soon found the route uphill and, having acquired a couple of loaves from a baker, made my way up the stiffly inclined road. I was now to retraverse the spine but at a point much further south than where I had originally begun.

Soon I had gained altitude and everything was panorama; I could distinguish an old tower on a hilltop looking black and sinister, and there was a long horizontal thread of villages just to the north of me. My direction was now towards Velanidia however, a settlement that marked the most south-eastern habitation of continental Europe. The way went up and the air cooled and became breezy and empty, no vehicles passed me although the track had been recently cleared. At last my feet were fitted to their shoes and to walking, my water was soon all gone though and I was constantly on the lookout for a cistern but the region was totally deserted, there were not even any flocks of goat. It was desolate, and once over the crest, the hills levelled to an undulating plateau, barren of anything but an occasional snake heating itself up on the bare road. There were not even any pitiless eagles wheeling about the dense air.

At last, by about mid-day, I saw the sea again, and there was a small church up ahead. The architecture of the churches down there was unlike that of the area about Monembasia or Zarax: they were less curved and more planar, less Byzantine it seemed. The one at Elaphonisos had been elegant, out on a headland next to the harbour, surrounded by mature cedars, a tree not indigenous to the region. I reached the church and found a tank of water from which I gorged like an animal, and leaving my stick and bag entered the chill of the building. The atmosphere inside was aromatic with frankincense and deliciously frigid after the burning hills outside. I sat for a long time, resting, letting my eyes adjust to the obscurity and then exploring the frescoes high up on the walls and about the dome. There was an excellent concave Pantokrator upon the central cupola.

For an hour or so I lay on a stone wall that enclosed a big old pepper tree to the side of the church. Walking in the heat of noon was like being struck with bars of lead and I felt heady. Several times I drank deeply from the tank and refilled my bottle; the volume of noise from cicadas was a terrific monotone, all the hills were alive with that intense rasping. I set off later as the sun moved down towards the west and shadows began to appear, thrown out by the hills, and reached the village by evening, a gathering of contiguous white houses that clung to the land above an open unsheltered bay. Tired, I went down to the water and found a spot far along the beach, and stripping off, dived in and swam for an hour, far out from the shore. What a joy that was, to be cool and wet, rather than stinking of sweat and covered in pallid obsolete dust.

By fortunate chance I had thrown my rucksack down beside a spring of water which must have been one of the few such sources in the whole province; and the small trickle and pool the size of a large bowl allowed me to stay there without having to wander in search of replenishment. I also discovered a small quantity of iron ore nearby, or what was possibly the detritus from an ancient smelting. My friend Dimitri, the patriarchal farmer who used to bring me tomatoes at Limonas, would often offer me such lumps of mineral, telling of how primaeval they were and how he had uncovered them on his land. Somewhere in one of my trunks here in Cambridge that piece of iron has settled.

From that base I explored the region, each day after waking and swimming and shaving and after reading some Shakespeare; by then I had gone back to Lear again, fascinated by the sublime majesty of the old king in his wilderness. Each day I would set off just with my cane, having stowed my bag under some myrtle, and wandered the paths of the area, then returned to sleep in the afternoon and to swim again. I must have spent two weeks like that but by then, time was beginning to blur and I was unaware of exacting chronology. I kept a notebook, writing in it of a morning and evening and that too is presently in a trunk of collected papers, folios, and early documents which I have not opened in a long time; it lies somewhere in one of the low unlit rooms of the attic. It was a trunk which I had acquired many years before when a student in Scotland and which was now bound tight with a blue P & O strap that I have owned since boyhood.

Each day I would visit the town to buy some bread; there was no baker there and the bread was brought by the postman in his van from Neapolis. There was not much of it and I lived for the main part on tea-biscuits and on the figs which grew plentifully about the village. There was one small café where each noon I permitted myself the relief of an orange soda, which I drank at a small green metal table in the only room of the place. That was like a drug, it was so sweet and cold and satisfying, but the bottles were minute and they never lasted long. Most of the houses of the village were shuttered and closed; the families had gone up to the Piraeus—I was told by the woman who ran the café—from whence the men worked on ships of the Hellenic Line.

At the centre of the town, close under the cliffs, were long stone channels and tanks in the shade of plane trees where formerly women had come to launder clothes, to gossip, and to take the good fresh water that flowed from a copious source. It was silent now and deserted except for beetles and mosquitoes. I loved that shady spot, there was an enchantment and a happiness about it, and one could almost hear the chatter and conversation from the vanished lives and the rinsing of the water. What is it that actually perpetuates itself in time, I wonder; does human consciousness ever leave a trace or do we only invent this out of desperation?

At night as I lay on my ground-sheet and sleeping bag I watched the heavens pass over gently through a cyanine darkness, the air fresh and saline. Ships were passing, running to or from the Piraeus or perhaps going up towards the Black Sea and Istanbul or over towards the Levant; further south I could discern the lights of vessels and hear their motors as they crossed the Mediterranean East-West, making passages between the Atlantic and Indian oceans. To the south was Crete and then Africa.

Sometimes, during the day, families of expatriate Greeks would come to play on the beach speaking American or Australian. Once or twice young men from those groups drew me into conversation, curious as to what I was doing and where I was from in the world. One afternoon when I had first arrived, as I was returning from a walk back towards the beach, I had found myself following in the way of three youthful women, their arms linked and their summer skirts swaying as they walked and their sandals clicking. As I passed them one exclaimed with shock, "A stranger!" "Yes," said another. "Look at his arm," a third commented. On my left arm, above the elbow, I wore a large ivory ring given to me by a travelling companion long ago in the Congo. I always wore it, for when I had first put it on I had been ill with malaria and was terribly thin; now it would not come off and I still have it on today, after forty years. "Well," said the second young lady, "It means that he is married," to which they agreed with *ahhs* and *hmms*. On other occasions, as I passed through the village after a day's walking, as families were rising from their siestas I would be invited in to drink a coffee or be offered a plate of food. Their eyes were always curious as to my white bracelet, but no one ever actually inquired.

Day after day of silently patrolling the region, I began to feel constrained by the lack of conversation and began to feel disoriented, lost from any purpose; being alone and friendless within an empty topography requires a particular fashion of mental discipline and my dreams at night beside the quietly unrolling waves were extraordinarily dramatic. Sometimes in the hills I would meet a shepherd with a few goats or a man tending to some olives, but the region was harsh, poor, and treeless. There were a lot of big snakes that would fly away at my approach, so swift were they it seemed that they were not even touching the ground. Once a nun on a donkey passed me and was astounded. "Where are you from," she asked with great humility. "Are you an angel?" She gave me a cucumber from her saddlebag which was delicious and I consumed every morsel of it for walking in these hills of an afternoon was a thirsty practice. Only now and again would I come across a broken cistern full of near-stagnant water, there were no wells. Occasionally there would be a ruined farm-house, surrounded by abandoned wooden implements, all jettisoned it seemed; I never came across any metal tools. Once or twice I would find a bare chapel, silent except for the knocking and booming of a fluent wind about its walls. Curiously, the icons in those chapels had inscriptions not in Greek but in a Cyrillic script, for the Ottomans had once colonised the area with Serbs.

My gathering *angst* was only tempered by the extraordinary beauty of the area. Sometimes on my walks I would stop on a hill and gaze out at the hard dry land, the rock and argent light. It was an intense but overwhelming beauty with something of the prophetic about it; the sun was so fierce and strong and the noise of cicadas, when there was shrubbery, was unbelievably loud and static. The sea about and below was a pure fire of simmering opaline leaves, flickering and coruscating without perspective or level, without horizon; there was no distinction between ocean and light. That was the most beautiful sight of all and I would find myself a patch of shadow from a rock or almond tree and simply watch for hours, lost in thought.

I had heard from my old chum Dimitri about a German look-out station constructed somewhere in these parts for the invasion of Crete in Nineteen

Forty-one. That had been the first airborne invasion in which gliders and parachutists—all young men, almost boys—had been used. The Cretans shot many of them out of the sky as they floated down and the battle had been arduous and the Allies were only defeated after several days of onerous fighting. A town to the north of Monembasia had provided the Germans with their aerodrome as it was situated on a great plain of olive and citrus. Even today that long straight runway remains, although now it is a road and lined with eucalyptus trees. That was from where the gliders, freighted with their cargoes of novice parachutists, set off towards Crete.

I had asked several times in the village of Velanidia as to the location of this building and if there were paths going towards it. "Over there," was all the direction I ever received, along with a gesture towards the south. There were no paths in that area although day after day I searched, my calves and ankles torn and scratched by thorn and loose stones. Eventually however I did find the building, two rooms of brick and rock with concrete floors; the roof was gone, it had probably been of metal, and there were bits of wood from window frames lying about. It was all visibly wrecked though but wonderfully sited.

Dimitri had always told me to find the place and buy it and make it into a home; his wife had come from Velanidia and he had known the site well. Often I would go there of late afternoon and sit and watch the sea. Sometimes a ship would cross over the distance as the water and the light fused with a brilliant and dazzling vitality that was a joy to perceive. Sometimes I could just hear those young German voices caught up in a war far away from their northern cities and green wooded fields; there was the crackle of a wireless and the sound of aero-engines, hundreds of motors passing above.

Dimitri had once told me of a German aircraft shot down off Monembasia by a British fighter and how as a boy he had watched the duel. All those futile young lives, lost and tormented in battle, but it had been the civil war that occurred after the war against the Axis which had destroyed more Greek lives in this part of the country: Communists fighting again Royalists, killing each other night after night and burning each others' houses. In Richea, the feuding had been exceptionally bitter and my wife had heard stories of Russian roulette being played on captives and there were photographs of decapitated heads lined up on a wall. I wondered how those horrific experiences were ever forgotten; was it actually possible to disconnect such filaments and moments of time, of memory or did the metonymy of violence persist like some terrible infection.

Now the hills were naked, dust and stones and light were all that stayed, herb and thorn moving in ways that were undetectable to human perception. The cape of Maleas was close, toward the south, but for some reason I never ventured down there; I do not know why, but I never did. I looked many a time in that direction for a path, but perhaps tired of the isolation and intimidated, I never ventured that far south, not there at least. I was becoming jaded and my zone of patrol never reached that way; it was as if I had done enough and my tenacity was flagging and uncompanioned solitude was beginning to overwhelm me.

On that shore at Velanidia I read and reread many times the poem *Mythistorema* by George Seferis. It was a poem that I had always loved and I had purchased a small card-bound copy in Neapolis. It is a poem about journeying and travel, about how a language and its imagery moves through time and collects us during that progress. The sea is very much part of its narration, the oars, islands, and sails.

Years later when I was living in Cambridge and working on my second book, *Eros*, that poem as I had read it on the shore repeatedly during so many afternoons—sitting under the terrific sun in the shelter of a large boulder which had disinterred itself from the cliff above and fallen onto the sand—that poem continued to filter through me. Although I had been on foot and walking, my journey and way were similarly immaterial, unfounded and noetic. In Cambridge there was no walking, there was no landscape to the urban environment, and instead I had taken to sculling on the river: up and down, day after day in a racing shell, occasionally competing. Under the bridges I went, along the banks with their various birds, heron, egret, cormorant, swan, goose, and in May the swallows like azure darts; and there were of course always the crows and the hawks at eternal war with each other. Rowing for me replaced walking, and the images of *Mythistorema* often came back to me whilst I was out there on the water.

Eros was a book about a similar kind of mental journey, especially as it involved love: the metaphor of human love, its lucidity and universality, its vicissitudes, and ultimately, its lack of reciprocity for it is possible for impassioned lovers not to actually be friends. It was a journey that had no project but only movement, lacking a fundamental efficacy or fruition. This was both myth and story, as in the Seferis poem, a stream of water upon which we moved and which we were always trying to drink from, and yet, to which we were never fully able to surrender our thirst. It was then when I began to comprehend the priority not of love but of friendship.

During those walks in Morea over the years and particularly during that walk about the region of Maleas, I observed, in my mind's eye, many a lion and lioness—hence the title of another small book that I wrote—although no one ever believed me. They always came in the evenings after the sun had settled, slowly pacing the hills in pairs, the same topaz colour as the earth itself. In fact my wife and son used to joke about such creatures, "O yes," they would say sometimes, "Don't you see the lions?"

It was with a certain relief that one morning I left the bay, but also with a slight melancholy, for I knew that I would never be so ruthlessly balanced as that again, so inspired and unknown and weightless. The day I left I found a small piece of a broken oar, still with bits of green paint inside the grain that had not been dissolved by the sea. I took that with me, that and the lump of raw iron; somehow they reminded me of the plainsong of Thucydides and his understanding of the long past and historical tragedy.

As I walked up the oblique road my head felt heavy and clouded; I could not quite focus my eyes in the intense sunlight. By then it must have been early July and the Dog Days, *Canicules*, and it was absolutely hot and bright. The light was so strong as to almost seem black and two-dimensional and I had difficulty walking, my skull was full of shadow and my eyes would not adjust properly. Once over the ridge I diverted to the north a little to where a huge old umbrella pine stood apart. In that shade I collapsed and slept for hours and when I awoke it was dark. I stayed the night there rousing early but was confused as to where I lay, unable to understand why there was no sea before me to walk into and wash. My body was sore from sleeping not on sand but on pine needles and pebbles. In fact I was woken by a tugging at my arm, and realised that a large fat yellow centipede had stung me and was attempting to withdraw its doubled-fanged tail from my flesh. The wound ached for hours.

I set off back towards the south again but kept away from Neapolis, staying high, and followed a track that led towards Maleas. I passed a small village—it must have been a Sunday—where groups of men sat outside a café beneath an awning, drinking coffee and playing backgammon. I could hear the click of dice and counters as I walked by under their stern inhospitable gaze, for no one likes a slack wanderer.

Soon I was in another kind of terrain, a broad area between sea and mountain upon which gigantic boulders were casually strewn as if by the hand of a titan. They must at one point have disengaged from the hillside, probably during an earthquake, and rolled down onto the flat. They appeared metaphysical in their achromatic isolation and cast elliptical shadows. The land about was untypical insofar as it was dry grass without shrub or tree; it was as if the area had once been cultivated and had now reverted, yet nothing had seeded and there were no walls nor terracing. Something was not quite right about the topography—spatially it was different—it was not quite natural and yet it was certainly not human. Here and there a prickly pear threw out its weird arms.

My map gave no indication of anything in this area south of the hamlet that I had just passed through. I did not know where I was going but nevertheless a path, and quite a good path, led south; I kept to this. All day I followed that way as slowly the mountains to my left came down closer to the sea and gradually the thin track rose upward and became confined—sometimes less than a foot in breadth—clinging to the hillside far above the waves below. Everything was livid stone and rock, there was no vegetation and to my right the Aegean was a crackling ultramarine, hot and sparkling and profoundly blue. The path became more precipitous and I found myself leaning towards the hillside in an effort to keep away from the drop. It was a good path though, clear of stones and soft with powdery dust. I was grateful for my stick then, carrying it companionably in my left hand.

Towards late afternoon I could just distinguish some buildings up ahead. By then the path was high above the water and the rise on my other hand was formed of large impassable shale; there was no alternative but to press on. Finally I came to a formal wrought-iron gate set into a stone arch. This I opened and entered, feeling trepidation as to what might be waiting for me as I came to a row of low houses, single rooms set against the hill, and a chapel mounted on a raised dais to the other side with a campanile and bells. Below, the cliff fell perpendicularly hundreds of feet into the ocean.

What I had arrived at was a small monastery but no one was there. I dropped my bag and stick and found the cistern, and, careful of somnolent snakes, threw in the bucket and drank, then stripped and doused myself. Next, I explored the rooms which were unlit and unfurnished except for low wooden beds neatly made up with sheets and blankets. On shelves there were glass jars of honey and coarse dried bread. Everything was clean and tidy, uncannily so and strangely motionless.

Outside again, I sat down on a stone ledge that ran the length of the houses and rested in the shadow. The remoteness of the place felt strange and I felt like an interloper for it was as if I should not have been there. It was like some of the hermitages that my friend and I had come across up on Athos, but they had been ruinous and overgrown; here everything was stark and dry and proper. I began to feel that I was in the company of invisible people: they could not see me and I could not see them, but we were both aware of each other. I also kept on noticing at the margins of my sight, white birds; but they never actually seemed to be there when I inspected more closely. It was very odd.

Beside the cistern a lemon tree was in bloom with sweet milky flowers and I kept on thinking that there were birds rustling among the foliage.

The spot was beautiful, possibly the most exquisite *locale* I had ever visited in Greece; it was stunning in its situation and spectacular in its severity. Yet I did not feel easy, something was unquiet about the vicinity, with its poise and exclusion. Inside the chapel the icons were hung with much gold jewellery, rings and bracelets and chains as well as dozens of silver votive plaques. The icons were all dedicated to Agia Eirene: Saint Irene, goddess of Peace. I lit three candles and sat for a while in the pale blue silence, my mind dazed by the day's extreme progress and my hydration levels were not yet restored; I felt dizzy and drunk and my head was ringing.

Outside the sun had gone over the edge of the next peninsula, that of Mani, which I had walked around one November many years before. Shadows were creeping out from the mountain and its prohibitive rocks. The sunset over Mani, far away in a vague distance, was picturesque with a gigantic sky above where a new young moon soon exposed herself, thin and lissom, lying upon her back and tinted with magenta. I recalled those days when I had walked there, for I had not liked those villages which were in fact fortified towers. They were incredibly beautiful to see, with a sharp ascendant geometry, but the spirit of conflict and antagonism I found unattractive. I had done that walk in the same year that I had met my wife, in fact we must have met a month or so after the journey. It all seemed so far away that evening, physically distant in space and time. Agia Eirene was high and unattached as to seem nearly projected into the heaven; all was atmosphere and pure abstraction.

I passed an uneasy night in one of the cells, waking frequently and thinking that I could hear voices or footfall, and feeling that I was being physically examined; it was not a good night and my dreams were peopled with vague figures treading about. The next morning I was up before it was light and although there was no moon the radiance from the stars was plentiful and sufficient for me to wash and shave at the cistern. The darkness was clear, transparent and enveloping.

I breakfasted on hard bread and honey and some olives that I had with me from Velanidia and drank a lot of water. I still did not feel relaxed but the vehement aesthetic of the place and its intense tranquillity was something I could not quit. Wandering about I noticed a set of stone steps going down to the water and carefully descended, and there, upon a platform right on the sea, was an ancient, unwhitewashed and unfaced chapel. It was old, Twelfth century or earlier, Byzantine, and it had no door.

At first I did not go in, but sat on the stone bench outside. The platform was only a foot or so above the waves which sank deeply down without gradation. It reminded me of the verticality of a reef that I had once stayed on in the Red Sea with my travelling companion who had given me the ivory band; we had gone there to dive and lived for several weeks on the surrounding basis of a lighthouse which the British had built. Its tall cylinder was then manned by three unspeaking Sudanese. Outside the reef Kim and I had swum down each day to watch the sharks below in the deep. Here at Maleas—I don't know what it was—but I was certainly not going to enter that water; swimmer that I was, I knew that it was too dangerous, but I did not know why; the solitude and its strangeness troubled me. It was not a fear of the submarine, but something else much more indefinite and I felt like I was on the verge of life, of its periphery. It was not a good feeling and I felt foolish and naive to be so discomfited; I do not think that I have been so alone and friendless in my life.

The shelf was slightly damp from the water, for the sun was not yet high enough to have touched the spot. The sound of the swell lapping at the stone was pleasant and the air had a moist marine odour that was pleasing. After a while I entered the chapel down a short passage, straight and dim and it was as if one were entering a cave, doorless and thickly walled. Inside it was humid and the sound of waves was magnified by the volume as the low sound oscillated back and forth percussing the surfaces. Slowly my eyes adjusted to the inspissate light, and slowly I discerned, hovering in the air about me against the black, figures in green and dark blue, crowned and with swords and lances in their hands, staring in neutral and impossible silence, their colourless amber eyes unblinking and their bodies breathless.

I do not know how long I stood there, barefoot and shirtless, gazing back at those tall bearded grey creatures. I could hear an intonation, paratactic, monadic, and low, a murmur that was inhuman and unearthly, it was a sound beyond what might be described as entrancing, was inaudible and yet perceptible. For long we stood gazing at each other, I forget how many there were of them, hovering in the air above me.

Later on that morning when I had retreated back up the staircase and was sitting on the ledge again outside the cells, absorbing and admiring the serenity of the place, I began to grow used to the strange concentration and yet the utter vacuity of my situation. I felt comfortable at last and I passed a couple of days there, alone and yet knowing that I was not without company on that solar promontory. The nights were always complicated however, with shadows and quiet inquiry.

On several occasions I was called to attention by a tanker or container-vessel far below which had steamed in close to the cliffs and was blowing a foghorn. Over a loud-hailer a captain or first officer would call up, "Eirene, Agia Eirene, Agia Eirene." Initially I had been bewildered and perplexed by this, unsure as to whether I should show myself, but then I threw on my shirt and went and waved and the ship hooted back. The next time this happened I put on my shirt and went and pulled the lines that ran up to the bells causing a delightful tintinnabulation to ring out and echo among the rocks. The captains liked that and would hoot three times before heading their vessels off towards the west. I realised that they must be Greek ships bound towards the Americas or Europe, if not further, and were putting in for the blessing of the saint, Our Lady of Pilots.

I passed numberless days at Agia Eirene and then one morning, having slept in a stupor once again and woken distracted, something happened which I am unable describe as it was absolutely visual. I immediately left the place, returning along the thin precipitous path.

Later, years later in Cambridge, perhaps it was in the writing of William Leake, whose wonderful book, *Travels In The Morea*, I read and reread closely, I came across a reference to Maleas. Perhaps it was in the writing of another early traveller, I cannot exactly recall the reference now. Colonel Leake had been in Athens when it was a Turkish village in the early Nineteenth century when Byron had been there and had worked as a British agent during the Napoleonic wars and had been preparing a cartography of southern Greece. I admired his prose immensely and had even gone to the length of acquiring an original edition. He, or whoever it was, described sailing past the hermitage on that cliff, the promontory of Maleas, and looking up and seeing a solitary recluse, a hermit, who had waved and rung the bells of the church. He was apparently famed for his enlightenment.

 I returned to Neapolis and stayed a night in my former miniscule windowless room. It was a strange experience to sleep among people, to promenade along the sea-front of an evening in the company of amorous couples and families and to sit at a café table and to read a news-paper and to write letters. It felt unreal and yet I was relieved to be among human society again and to post off correspondence toward friends.

Setting off again with first light, I was back on the route up towards the hills. By now I was fatigued and had walked enough and the region had entered inside me; I no longer observed much of what existed before my eyes. Also, my experiences down on Maleas bore a certain completeness about them; nothing else could quite possibly exceed that and I felt fulfilled in a way that I cannot express except in poetry. It had been something like Dante's experience at the focus of the *Paradiso*. Dante had, of course, made his journey on foot for he too had been a walker except for when Santa Lucia flew upward with him in her arms from Purgatory. The poet says, *Un punto solo m'è maggior letargo che venticinque secoli a la 'mpresa che fé Nuttuno ammira l'ombra d'Argo*; for at that point nothing can be spoken.

I made my way towards an outcrop that sprang from the plain and where the ruins of a Byzantine or Ottoman fort stood. There I spent a few hours pottering about looking for anything that might give me some indication of date—potsherds or bits of metal—but I found nothing apart from some round leaden bullets which I did not keep. The walls were of umber stone, unlike the rock of the area, and there was an air of disharmony about the site, of force or cruelty, which I did not like, and I left.

That day the *Caniculae* were unbearable and I had not gone far when the steel mallets of the sun were crashing down upon my temples again and I retreated into a low tubiform chapel and fell asleep on the cold terracotta floor, waking only at dusk. I made it as far as the umbrella pine that day and spent the night there again. By then my thoughts were turning homeward towards Monembasia.

The following morning I made a northerly way, following a good track towards where a series of three villages were strung out laterally against the hillside. There were dogs about and a few donkeys and goats and some shy children. The houses themselves were decrepit, with low arched doors below the level of the road and crude heavy lintels that covered diminutive windows. They were not attractive villages having a quality of the primitive about them and of rawness that lacked the mild zaniness which Greek villages usually exhibit. Even at the height of summer there were pools of fetid water lying about and large iridescent flies flitting above them. There was something disorderly and meagre about this settlement and I walked on without halting to chat or to ask for water. Decades later these hamlets were to be destroyed by summer fires and those ancient buildings ruined and horribly blackened.

I cannot remember where I slept that night, somewhere up on the plateau, rising early and continuing before the sun came from out of the sea; it was scorched and desolate up there but cooler than the plain below. I seemed to walk aimlessly for days and lost my way a couple of times among the stones and carob trees and had serious trouble with some shepherd dogs once. That was a nasty experience, for ferocious dogs are the hell of walkers. My momentum was failing, I was no longer impelled as I had been and the walk was coming to an end. Fortunately I was able to find water, often foul and insipid, and I had enough olives and bread and biscuits to keep me going.

At one point I was high above an inlet where two youths, shepherd boys—one much older than the other—were grazing their flock. I could hear their laughter and voices amplified by the valley in which they were encapsulated. Against that sound was the slow steady play of waves upon a hard shore. Not long after that I reached the settlement of Kastaneia, named after chestnut trees which I could not find. At a house I stopped for a glass of cold water, several in fact, and chatted with some men. One of them had a parrot on his shoulder whom he obviously adored; he was a sailor and the parrot was from Chile. It had a woman's name, something like Coco, and both man and bird were perfectly matched friends. He pointed me towards me the start of a path that I had taken some years before but had forgotten, which ran from a village just south of Limonas to this village. Now I was bound in a home direction and my walk was coming to its conclusion—if walks are ever concluded—for in our hearts we always continue long after events themselves are closed.

That part of the walk was sharp and prickly and my ankles were superficially scathed; I was also tired, something that I had not experienced since the outset of my journey. It was a profoundly internal exhaustion, a weariness of days and their excess of solitude, and I also suffered from a slight confusion and was reckless for companionship and any intimacy. I was becoming confounded and had lost my concentration and sensitivity, was not aware of my environment any more, everything was becoming unified. I had begun to long for those temperate days of late October when one first pulls on a sweater in the evening: the sensation of wool and the weight of the garment was something that preoccupied my thoughts. That, and the idea of shutting windows at night as the temperature fell outside, of sleeping in a double bed under blankets, of the smooth warm of a somnolent friend beside one.

On that final leg I saw no person nor any animals except for lizards except at one point as I skirted a valley I noticed an old man and a child resting beneath an arbutus tree taking their afternoon siesta as the cicadas roared about them. By late afternoon I was back on the track below Limonas where I had often walked in the evenings after work and it was pleasurably familiar. I slept on a beach near to the house that night as the house itself had been let to tenants for the rest of the summer. There were squills growing in the sand and beginning to bloom. That was my last time out under the sky and beside the water.

In the morning after ablutions I walked back along the road towards Monembasia. Looking down as I passed Limonas I could see a car parked outside with children and their many things; all was busy. I passed houses where people greeted me and asked where I had been. Sophia—the German girl who lived with a fisherman—was not at home and her house with its red metal roof and wind-blown pine tree looked empty, for they must have been out with their nets. Slowly I moved back into the familiar, the social and cultural, back from sole extremes: this was pleasurable. I visited Lolovania, the house that my wife had designed, and stayed there a night and then spent some days in rented accommodation out on Monembasia rock, as Lolovania too had resident guests. There, inside a courtyard with a pomegranate tree and within small vaulted rooms darkened with cotton sheets against the light and heat, I typed up my notes. Then, having discarded my filthy and broken canvas plimsolls I bought a new pair of sandals and took the ferry up towards Hydra and friends, to sleep inside walls or out on terraced roofs and to spend days in gentle and pacific conversation.

Soon my family arrived and I met them in Athens and we revisited Hydra and then returned to Monembasia for the winter. I had a vile spike of malaria at Christmas and by January we had changed our plans and were flying back towards Boston, *via* London.

After that I did not return to Greece for many years; it was too much. It would have been like seeing an old lover again and not knowing what to say. Having experienced such intimacy and closeness with a landscape I could not simply pay a casual visit, it was not possible. My wife and son would go back each summer and visit Richea and stay at Lolovania or perhaps at Limonas, but I only went back twice: once, on my fortieth birthday, prior to taking up the study of Sanskrit literature, and another time when I went with my son to lecture at various archaeological sites, which was work and in a way so different.

Then some years ago I returned alone and stayed at Lolovania. I had turned fifty, and to celebrate that event I crossed over to Turkey, going *via* Lesbos, and swam the Hellespont in imitation of Byron. Back in the Lakonic, I met up with my wife and we spent time driving about the area in a hired car with the friends who owned Limonas. It was a curious feeling for me to see all those places again and not to be on foot and I felt fully decadent. As Greece was now a member of the EU there were many more roads and often they were metalled. No longer was I alone and pedestrian but with friends and so everything—perception, effort, emotion, and accomplishment—all changed as the world became amplified and improved; there was no longer any ascetic and solitary medium to the light. One no longer slept naked on the sand at night, beside the waves.

One morning we drove across the hills to Neapolis and then back again towards Velanidia. How it transpired I do not know, but we ended up, after lunch, driving down a bumpy new track to the south of the village for several kilometres and parking. Then, having spoken with a shepherd about Maleas and being told, accompanied by vigorous signals, that there was now a path running to the lighthouse down there, we set off. I presumed that by lighthouse he meant the small sanctuary that I had formerly stayed at; it did not occur to me that they were separate places. I was excited because, for some reason during my long walk in the early Eighties, I had not explored this particular area. It was the sole part of the peninsula that I had not walked and suddenly it was as if I was finally completing the earlier peregrination and only now was true closure to be achieved.

The path was good but long and we miscalculated the distance, for at each successive headland we thought the cape would appear, but it did not. It was a strange day for there was no shadow and although it was hot the sky was filmed with a cast of cloud. It was also silent except for a heavy sea breaking over the rocks far below us, foam rising and falling over a jagged brown littoral. Nor did we have much water, which was a problem. At last there was the lighthouse, the most south-eastern tip of Europe: but we were on the other side of Maleas and Agia Eirene must have been around the point.

The lighthouse was an appealing piece of architecture, nearly Palladian and built of finely rendered stone. The shaft was domed with copper plate and had a finely cut metal wind vane. The rooms below were abandoned and covered in dust and fallen plaster, even the beds were littered with refuse. The place had a strangely forsaken feel to it as if the keepers had left in a hurry. Even the logbook of hours, the account of the lamp and its times of operation, had been left open on a table and I guiltily took one of those pages as a treasure for my notebook. At the top of the tower, three tremendous lenses surrounded the bulb and its massive cast-iron mechanism had corroded to a green patina of stiffness. The building was both lyrical and wistful, with an air of sudden dereliction that was eerie.

I would have liked to have stopped there for some days but it was not possible. We did not stay long as it would have been dangerous to be caught out on that path without a torch and without a moon. Returning we made swift time and arrived back below Velanidia at the onset of darkness and drank deeply at a spring, pouring water over each others' heads and laughing.

I was elated, for finally the walk was over and I was at liberty from all those numberless ideas and images generated by my walks about the territory. My relationship with the Morea had attained its equilibrium and was no longer passionate and impulsive, and one was among friends: that was the invisible and priceless key which had opened the final gateway and no longer did one have to endure and persevere alone. That was the jewel now hidden in my clasped hand like some wonderful and uniquely secret ruby.

Now, on the morning of the spring equinox almost forty years after I had first walked out—as the sun enters the house of Aries—I sit here at this old desk and the door bell rings and a postman hands me a padded envelope. Inside is a proof copy of my book, *Eros*, which contains the words inspired and formed by those walks in southern Greece. The first lines of the book, about a bird, were written one night in a taverna in Sparta when my wife and I had set out on that initial amorous stroll. We had been visiting Mystras, the ruins of the former despotate of the Morea high up above modern Sparta. The Turks had razed that upper city after an abortive attempt at independence in the Eighteenth century but the remains were still splendid and the frescoes were extraordinary. The last lines of the book were made after that final walk down to the lighthouse with our friends.

So now the walk—which had begun so many years before—was formally concluded. It was not simply a crossing of terrain but travel among the ideas constituted by that topography and my passages through it. The walk had been an interior journey, a transit among perceptions and feelings that had continued long after the physical trajectory was accomplished and often even far away from the actual situation itself. It was only in retrospect that the reality of the movement became truly perceptible: the truth about the substance of the place, about the nature of time, even about the activity of love and filial transaction, about the tissue which makes for human goodness and unity.

Morea had become intrinsic to my experience of all life, and was, in a sense, its essence and germ. *Eros* had originally had the title of *Unbecoming* but I had scrapped it on the advice of our companions as we had walked down to the lighthouse that afternoon. It was inappropriate, they said. For me, the idea of 'unbecoming' was phenomenological, it represented the negation of becoming and was a reversal or recollection. My walks down in Morea had been the constellation of a process which was in fact an *un*-becoming of ideas, that was the true progress involved: how they had revealed themselves to me in time. One had not been simply traversing a terrestrial plane but had in fact been in pursuit of certain thoughts and realisations which the material of the location had both informed and modified: the walk had been concerned with ideals in the Platonic sense and represented a retrieval of those forms of being. These had been graciously observed.

Landscape painting with its display of harmonious immobility—in many ways close to what still life painting also seeks to portray—offers a paradigm akin to the purpose of the walker, if his or her aim be true. One could propose that there is a moral dimension to walking in this way and that it can facilitate a possible virtue. The walker, in going away from the cultured world of causality, enters a natural world where origin, sequence, and narration, become less compelling. Simultaneity, in all its grandness of retardation, becomes the major tone—that of the a-temporal—in which our deepest and most sonorous being reveals itself as we *un*-become.

Sitting here at this small brown ash-wood desk with the two apple trees in the garden below being thrashed by an unseasonal north-easterly wind and the dogwood beneath the window being shaken about, I have been slowly re-assembling all the events and images of that walk, remembering step by step its serial form. One thing that I cannot recall is what shirt I wore as I set out that June morning, and all the connections which are linked to that shirt are thus lost. I know it was a white shirt from Edinburgh, but that is all I can remember; although, it might have been a blue linen shirt that my wife had once given to me as a birthday present in Cambridge. Memory functions by connection, by metonymy, but at some point when ends can no longer be attached to beginnings, continuity fails and we lose our way. Without company we cannot regain those impressions and so the sequence of life is lost and becomes simply a work of arbitrary *bricolage*.

Now, as I sit here in the late afternoon light which slants in low through the two deeply set windows—here among my Sanskrit dictionaries and the many manuscripts of my work on epic heroes—with the publication of *Eros*, walking in Morea is concluded. A long and complex cycle is done and now one glances about for those hints that will take one off again. How do we begin to set out, I wonder, how do we become recipient and impelled anew? What are those intimate connections, which although invisible, are always with us and of which we are unaware? I do wonder if human beings actually ever innovate or have original and new ideas for it appears that ultimately we just move from hand to hand.

~ On Friendship ~

II ~ III

THE friendship of women played a strangely outstanding role in the journey of the seafarer Odysseus. Once he had set aside the life of warrior culture—the ways and habits of violence and death—his voyage and return were to be thoroughly translated only according to the beneficence of women. For having desisted from and necessarily mourned the male and heroic world of martial conflict, Odysseus then proceeded according to speech and along paths of language: women, from Kalypso onwards, mediated those words. From the outset he was a *man without qualities* except for his intrinsic grief, although he was unaware of this emotion until it was aroused and vivified by the verses of the poet Demodokos with his first and third songs.

Curiously, in our present literature, Odysseus is without male friends in his poem, there are only women and then, his small family of wife and son. Even in the Homeric Iliad Odysseus demonstrates no friendly concerns: in Scroll X, Diomedes, with whom he crosses the lines at night, is certainly not a friend nor is he much of a companion, and in Scroll IX, the embassy scene, neither Aias nor Phoinix are bonded with Odysseus and clearly Achilles does not actually like him. In some tenuous non-poetic traditions Odysseus is a *nothos*, a 'bastard', and lacks even that usual agnatic connection; he certainly has no full siblings, which was uncommon for the time. Paradoxically he is alone yet always *polytropic* and what he represents is the paradigmatic exertion of a completely isolated human psyche towards creating association and affinity.

His journey homewards is also inexplicably complicated for this is a quadriform voyage, a narrative which recounts all that happened to the hero in four versions or dimensions of travel and explication; for not only is the hero mentally polytropic but also the medium of his voyage, the poetry itself is likewise multifold as too are the multitudinous vehicles of time. Firstly, there is the Homeric *Odyssey* writ large as it is touched upon during the twenty-four scrolls of the poem. Secondly, there is the travel as recounted in Scrolls v to xiii, where there are only three places given by the poets along that way: Ogygia, Phaeakia, and then Ithaka, during which time our hero travels solo. Then, there is the self-appointing journey as accounted by Odysseus himself during Scrolls ix to xii, depicting places otherwise not mentioned by the anonymous poets where his long excursion occurs *via* the tongue and declamation of Odysseus himself. In this representation Odysseus sings like a visionary poet telling of his many and personal courses and of his companionable crews.

Finally there is the micro-narrative of his complete journey given in the bedroom scene in Scroll xxiii as the lovers kiss and retire; this last account integrates the previous narratives into a single thread and it is as if memory coheres all that occurred into one plot: only in retrospection is the experience of time past at last incorporated and rendered reasonable. Curiously Poseidon is omitted from this series of events and the hero is depicted as a completely sole and authoritative agent: which is how Zeus speaks of human effort and volition in Scroll one.

As we know from Hesiodic poetry, the Muses who inspire poetry are endowed with an ability to deceive in order 'to make the false appear true', and once on his natal isle Odysseus becomes a prodigious fabricator and dissembler, just like his maternal grand-father Autolykos, famed for theft and perjury. The hero is both solitary and yet in that mendacious state he becomes countless; he is what I would describe as the perfect *femme fatale*, always pretending and inventing himself on each occasion for he possesses no nuclear nor interior self.

As a corollary to this, the *agonistic* relation which Odysseus endures with the outraged and vengeful Poseidon evinces a touching quality of this kind of unique psyche: for in the Homeric Iliad, in Scroll XIII, Poseidon himself impersonates several heroes and speaks most eloquently and deceptively in misleading mimicry of their voices; he too is a gifted fraud.

The amity of women in the Odyssey is crucial in these verbal exchanges or transactions which Odysseus makes and it is femininity that is the core element and medium of his progress and the real terrain of his mental and social movement. Women qualify his essential friendships for in all his journeying it was not so much the case that the unfamiliar allowed him an access to a familiar which is not otherwise available at home, but that the feminine engaged his mind in a manner that was both vital and compelling and constitutive of a renewed self. Along the roads towards home it was the feminine which cohered and imparted novel consciousness to the hero.

Hence Kalypso facilitates his art of shipbuilding and supplies him with the instruments of this and the young Nausikaa and her mother Areté are important in expediting his transportation back towards Ithaka where Eurykleia and Penelope recognise him and enable his reclamation of estate and status. Athene—also cunning and always disguised—is constantly at his side mentoring him in one way or another. It is the nymph Kirke who assists him in visiting death, that is, according to what Odysseus says, in his mid-voyage and then later, it is Ino who saves him from the waves. Even in the Underworld, Odysseus speaks with his mother and closely observes the *catalogue of women*, familiar with their lives and affinities and imitating how they speak; and it is the ambisexual Teiresias with whom the hero converses in Hades, who offers him prophetic advice.

What is it about womanhood that is so crucial for this man or men in general, what do they know which is so vital for the organisation and structure of the male psyche? How do these exchanges differ from what occurs between men and do there exist two differing kinds of amicable necessity, like water and food, the uniform fluid and various substance? Is it a metonymy or embodied lineage with an abstract maternity which is constantly being re-enacted and replayed or is it that the language of women is more significant in constituting male consciousness than the words of menfolk and there is a temporal dimension to such constitution? I use the terms male and feminine in a metaphorical sense here as indicative of the dichotomy of psychic principles and not so much as signs designating anatomy.

Given the model of this late bronze age poem can one aver that the words of the feminine are primarily generative of metonymy in language whilst the male principle of human amity supplies an act of substitution to human consciousness? Metaphor is like rainfall upon grass insofar as it promotes and impels growth whereas metonymy is like sunlight and in creative or prototypical sequence the latter will always precede the former.

The epic poem obviously makes it plain that the axis which occurs between the estranged hero and women is the most formally charged human nexus that is available to Odysseus as he seeks to refound and to re-formulate a cognitive individuality. From being alone and nobody the hero proceeds *via* feminine amity and speech towards his penultimate status as king, husband, and father. He sleeps with three of these informative women and at the close of his life he simply and pacifically returns to the sea, at a place where the usual signs of his life are no longer recognised.

In this narrative it is as if the horizontal or structured axis of being is composed according to feminine communication and the male axis is formed according to more diachronic relations: the women replicate whilst the men systematise in serial vertical hierarchy. It is the latter which removes men from only self-awareness, something which Odysseus—at last reconfigured as a king and no longer a warrior—must retrieve if he is ever to travel homeward with integrity. It is telling, in this light, that all the friendships which Odysseus incurs are with the feminine.

If a true journey concerns the unfamiliar and our conception here—according to this stamp of archaic and preliterate poetry—complies with a feminine form which substantiates the reasonable process taking place along that trajectory and scale, these then are the procedures which lead to an embodiment of consciousness.

For the knowledge that women have to offer men is not available elsewhere in that ancient culture; if the destiny of males was one of challenge and conflict, strife and competition, then that of the feminine concerned kinship and union, according to the dynamics of this poetic exemplum. I do not speak of physiology nor of sexual difference but of principles or intellectual nodes about which validity gathers and becomes coherent.

Like a *femme fatale* Odysseus is uniquely privileged in that he translates between this binary formulation of existence, admitting both obverse and reverse upon one plane. The most ancient deity Dionysos was a similar figure insofar as he too was constantly fluctuating among identities as he altered masks and subjectivity; but it is difficult to connect this deity and our hero as their narratives cannot be mutually transferred, for one is dramatic and the other is epic.

There exists a quality in the dialogue of friendship between a boy and girl—the male and feminine—that does not take place between any other like figures, in the unsaid or *phatic*: words as messages which are bound up with metonymy, allusion, and enigma rather than with a specific transmission of data. This *meaningless* axis lies at the heart of human awareness and transition and is the medium of our most fundamental psychic procedures and it was this complex and deeply involved medium which primarily informed Odysseus with his bearing of self, reconstituted from a warrior type that had only revolved about the undeviating skills and activities of violence and the innate companionship drawn from intimacy with death.

It was in his exchanges with women—in terms of speech, language, and constant interpretation—that enabled the consciousness of Odysseus to amalgamate such connotation about his core emptiness: these women with whom he spoke offered him certain templates of being which he adopted so that his potential might flourish and their phenomena become disclosed. In the view of the poem what women supply to men is an access to an ability to perceive the nature of likely attachment—especially in a linguistic sense—

something which in male relations is not always immediately present, being abstracted; and in epic poetry that abstract detachment concerns contention.

The polytropic and versatile Odysseus characterises metonymy in human form for his constantly unstable, labile, and protean nature exists in steady motion throughout a range of significance; unlike Achilles, Odysseus is unable to be naturally discrete. Achilles, in his poem refuses all metaphor and its coinage and he does not allow himself to enter into that economy of exchanges, whereas Odysseus is constantly a figure or voice of metonymy, as he communicates and deals his words and so becomes able to enter into a series of transactions. For Achilles there is only one unbreakable and inviolable metaphor and that is his *kléos áphthiton*, the 'imperishable fame' which only he has access to on earth; and in that light all other metaphors are irrelevant and lack any significance for him. The narrative contrast of this condition would be the experience which Odysseus shares with the Sirens where he becomes aware of their absolute knowing yet makes himself unable to react to such compelling information, whilst they are unable to effect any alteration in his psyche.

What is at work is an active and dynamic relation which occurs between pre-conscious awareness and the initial sign: that is the drama of Odysseus and in this sense—just as *mimésis* is prior to metonymy—so metonymy will always precede metaphor in terms of how consciousness is composed. It is the women whom he meets during the latter part of his journey and for whom he is a stranger that enables this adaptable and pliant *persona* to reify or constellate about what he means and finally intends to be. He is the master signifier of the poem and captain of meaning as he wanders among various truths and his voice becomes increasingly feminine until he eventually becomes king again through the profoundly successful archery competition in which there is no other contestant. In this and during this process he is totally receptive; again, this is completely unlike the psychic comportment of young Achilles.

All of the poem's narrative is so verbally connected to Odysseus and like the zero in numeration he conveys little intrinsic content except in combination where he changes all value; that is, until he regains his sceptre on Ithaka. Similarly, psyche is like that figure of nil which is so immensely transformative, puissant, and catalytic in any combination.

As Odysseus takes up his penultimate task of agonistic competition, the twang of his bow is likened to the sound of a swallow in spring. Suddenly, as an arrow is nocked and discharged, this bird announces the return of the husband and ruler, and from across the water fame is restored by the vernality of homecoming or *nostos*. That athletic event had been conceived and proposed by Penelope and offered as a challenge to the suitors; yet during her conversation with her mate on the night prior to that minute it had not been the voice of a swallow which signified change but the enigma of a talking eagle, a bird which the poets associate with both Zeus and Odysseus. This, she had carefully proposed as being representative of her returned husband. The intellection and emotion of Penelope so enabled the raptor to become a bird of passage forecasting a return of social and marital fertility; such was her private and discreet signal to him.

Metaphorically, in this model of archaic bronze-age culture, if women offer water and men exchange food, then male life concerns bloodshed, rituals of war, and conflict whereas the feminine world concerns all that circulates about the rites of marriage and connubial animation: this is the basic counterpoint. Menstruation is opposed to hunting, childbirth is in counterpoint to war, weaving is a mirror of archery, the shuttle and the arrow.

Odysseus is remarkable in that he is able—thanks to how women admit to his perpetual incongruity—to combine both traits into one song, both eagle and swallow, destroyer and creator. An irreducible asymmetry obtains between the male and feminine and it is an intermediary and metaphorical liquid that distinguishes women from men, in the same manner that the appearance of human labour distinguishes a mythical age of gold from an age of silver, and structurally—in terms of pattern although not duration—one precedes the other, just as metonymy precedes metaphor.

It is at his original point of solitude that the poet cues and urges the Muse to commence the song, when the hero is with Kalypso. Then, Odysseus, as a mariner, arrives sole and lone upon the Phaeakian shore and only then does he truly seek to return home and he does this primarily through poetic speech to a male audience and attentive listening to amicable women. Then it was the women who were able to offer to this stranger the necessary signals for complete travel, otherwise he is doomed to the transience of perpetual metonymy and unable to coin one metaphor of value which might become his own.

The ultimate challenge for Odysseus is thus to transfer from a condition of metonym to that of metaphor, for such is the instant which marks the origin of human understanding. For our hero, that mimetic action wherein one might observe the schooling of fish or the flocking of birds is long past and buried deep within an amorphous emotional record; only then is he able to cast off all semblance and his many disguises and so presume true authority.

In our poem what men say among men does not parallel what women speak among women, yet Odysseus the continual stranger fused this distinction between the feminine and non-feminine or the *strange*. It is a fusion that distinguishes the consciousness of civility and humanism, being that one mark of wisdom which is able to reprise our fragile humanity. Men are inherently foreigners and migrants on earth and in that lies their heroism but not their humanity, and in the abstract all culture derives and depends from this primary exchange which evolves between women and strangers and, in an hypothetical sense, this instant constitutes the germ and nucleus of likely friendship: the awakening of emotional judgement.

It is both notable and remarkable that the agonism which occurs between Achilles and Apollo in the Homeric Iliad, when one inspects the relations of Odysseus and that deity, Apollo is benign to the hero and Odysseus is reverential to the divinity. In terms of divine support there exists a profound and complex duality between Achilles and Odysseus, of antithesis and counterpoint, in their distinction of metaphor and metonym. It is telling that the contention between the two heroes—when one considers Apollo—is enacted as an antithesis to Achilles and an affinity with Odysseus. It is this kind of phenomenal dimension that lies at the heart of what we have been referring to as election. As Apollo is director of the Muses he is thus the source of all poetry in the *kosmos*.

The pilgrims, the *théoroi*, a term which supplies us with our word 'theory', are these men; they are the ones to communicate to us what they have seen, and being so able to communicate and find easiness with metonymy they are truly able to travel. It is only the feminine however, which is able to terminate that endless sea of transition, when men might at last become bound to the novelty of metaphor.

In true friendship there is a constant and recursive recognition of metaphor and an admiration for such exchanges and in this case virtue is like the streamlined altruism of truth, but a truth which is hypostatic. To cite the old adage, 'to navigate is necessary, it is not necessary to live'.

~ ON FRIENDSHIP ~

III ~ I

BETWEEN the Atlantic ocean and the Caribbean sea lie a group of small and once volcanic islands whose administrative centre is presently in Grenada; these are part of the larger cluster of Windward Islands, the Indies of the West. One of the lesser Grenadines, the isle of Carriacou—first spelled *Kayriouacou* in the Seventeenth century as a Carib word—was originally settled by Arawaks in the early centuries of the present era when they had migrated there in small boats, *canoua*, from the coast of South America. Their presence was later overwhelmed by the advent of Amerindian Caribs who were themselves later to be swallowed by the arriving Europeans. Ceramic debris from these two neolithic cultures are still to be found today on the coast of Carriacou hidden among mangrove sands; and one or two words from that proto-Amerindian language are still in use, such as *maniku*, 'opossum', and *tatu*, 'armadillo'. Nowadays Carriacouans often refer to themselves as *Kayaks*.

Carriacou is about twelve degrees north of the equator and sixty-two degrees west of Greenwich; it is a volcanic and limestone island of about thirty square kilometers. From the Seventeenth century onward the British and then the French took turns in contending for control of the Grenadines and Carriacou was controlled by France for a total of one hundred and seventeen years, between 1650 and 1763, and between 1779 and 1783. Even today, Protestant and Catholic denominations of the Christian church sustain a mild competition for souls on the isle. The Europeans brought men and women from West Africa as a work-force, from what are presently Dahomey, Guinea and the Congo, although the first African inhabitants of Carriacou came from

Guadaloupe, and not directly from continental Africa. Later, Scottish migrants established themselves on Carriacou in the Seventeenth century as boat-builders and many family or place names on the island remain Scottish today. In the town of Windward on the north-east tip of the isle the *bukra* people are still fair in complexion and eye-colouration and remain traditionally endogamous. About six thousand folk live on the isle at present yet many more Kayaks inhabit the cities of England and North America. The *patois* that is now spoken derives from French, English, and various African dialect stems.

Until secular modernity with its galloping consumerism arrived in the recent decades Carriacou was poor without electricity, roads, or schools. The older generation still recall a time when villages consisted of thatched or 'grass' houses built from mud and wattle. By Nineteen Thirty-eight the old system of estate ownership of land had almost vanished and more than half of land tenancy was made up of small-holdings, share-cropping or *metayage*, and squatting. The estates by then produced limes as a principal crop and cotton and corn were cultivated only by small-holders. That old system of customary tenancy is nowadays becoming more legalised and formal yet the actual and *real* holding of land—of buildings on the land and the usufruct of trees on the land—complicates this pattern. All these sub-surface social patterns of migration underlie the complex modes of human amity which occur and exist on this small island today.

During the early period of Independence—from Nineteen Seventy-four onwards, the Gairy years—Carriacou was systematically neglected by the metropolitan government in St. George's, Grenada, what is referred to as the *mainland*; everything, including food, was scarce during that time. Uncle Gairy disliked the Kayak island for it had not supported him during elections, preferring their own man, Herbert Blaize, who had been Premier in the years immediately prior to full Independence.

People still speak of the Revolution of Nineteen Seventy-nine when Maurice Bishop's New Jewel Movement seized control of the government and forced Gairy and his thuggish 'Mongoose Gang' into exile; that movement itself recalled a previous rebellion of the Eighteenth century led by the heroic Julien Fedon. There was an optimism during that revolutionary time which fuelled a populist and socially creative system and this period marked the beginning of the new Carriacou, an era marked by increasing migration away from the island and later, by the coming back of such newly affluent folk and by a general but slow increase in the tourist trade. The NJM *régime* was toppled by an invasion of US military forces in Nineteen Eighty-three who fought and destroyed Bishop's militia and established a fresh democracy.

Nowadays there is a small community of resident Europeans and North Americans who have themselves migrated to live on the isle. Trinidad and Venezuela are at present culturally closer in many ways than Florida and North America, and Cuba remains an important educational presence. Carriacou, as part of Grenada, is a member of the Eastern Caribbean Currency Union, which presently has its central bank on St. Kitts. The island is therefore—in terms of affinity—completely attached to other places, histories, and societies and keeps to no unitary separation of life.

The island is primarily covered with second-growth forest, mostly of acacia and some prickly pear. Sugar and cotton were some of the principal crops which the isle produced during those early years of agriculture; later, once the sugar market collapsed, limes were cultivated. A number of the trees which now flourish on the hills and many of the plants that grow there were introduced from the Pacific islands, thanks to the endeavours of navigators like Captain Bligh. He carried seeds and stock aboard his ship *Providence* in an attempt to develop what were then viewed as colonies: hence the breadfruit tree was brought in at the end of the Eighteenth century.

Many plant species—such as the Norfolk pine—had been first discovered by Captain Cook. Other kinds of tree, like the rubber tree and the laburnum, originated in India; the bottle brush was introduced to the islands from Australia and the travellers' tree derived from Madagascar. Thus not only society, but also the *flora* is a consequence of once alien admixture and the plant life of Carriacou is composed of so many diverse elements which nevertheless possess a comfortable kinship which is both naturally and aesthetically successful; these vegetative species are all thoroughly companionable. Since the latter Eighteenth century the biological pattern of the isle has moved from an original forest cover to the plantation of cash crops, to gardening, and then to pasturage for stock: these have marked the main topographic states and transitions, a natural movement within which so many varying species have successfully combined.

The climate is humid and tropical and the temperature varies little during the course of a year, typically remaining in the low eighties *fahrenheit*. Sometimes devastating hurricanes strike and demolish whole areas as trees and dwellings are levelled. The force of these tempests is immense and they destroy the livelihood of communities with brief ease; in one night, Hurricane Ivan, in the winter of Two Thousand and Four, removed most of the rooves of buildings on the island of Grenada, and wrecked most of the spice orchards, particularly the nutmeg groves. On Carriacou, the worst hurricane in living memory occurred in Nineteen Fifty-five, when Hurricane Janet caused horribly terrifying destruction and suffering; recovery took decades.

For many years during the second half of the Twentieth century Carriacou was poor and its economy derived essentially from fishing and subsistence gardening along with the minor production of livestock. Households subsisted by cultivating small patches of land for maize, peas, and roots, and there was little market for goods. Until the recent decades, there were few paved roads on the island, tracks were the only way and transport and movement were by donkey or on foot.

Water is a problem on Carriacou as there are no springs and the earth retains little of the capricious seasonal deluge; an intense cultivation of the terrain has never thrived even though there are typically more than forty inches of annual rainfall during the wet season. There has been much soil erosion— particularly on the windward side of the island—due to ill-conceived patterns of agriculture, especially cotton and the later cultivation of cash crops like ground-nut. Houses supply themselves with sufficient water by collecting rain in tanks and cisterns and during periods of drought village people will visit houses with larger cisterns in order to request assistance. Water for cattle and flocks can become crucial and the few ponds and catchment areas do not always suffice; water has even been imported from Grenada in the past during times of severe scarcity; a Chinese-built desalination plant that was constructed near Hillsborough no longer functions. The dry season, when the grass is scorched and fields turn a parched serum-yellow, prohibits any large-scale animal husbandry despite metropolitan policies that have fostered such kinds of livelihood.

Boat-building and smuggling or the *bobul* trade has long flourished and today on the nearby isle of Petite Martinique the running of contraband remains an essential activity for the local economy. Carriacou was once famed for its shipbuilding but the number of active shipwrights began to decline from the late Sixties and today boat-building is almost a *recherché* activity and much of the required timber is no longer indigenous but imported. There is nowadays a new effort to recapitulate that old marine tradition, the Vanishing Sail movement, which is slowly re-establishing the work of shipwrights upon the shores at Windward.

There is the curious demographic phenomenon, so common in much of the developing world today, where emigration over the decades has drastically altered the social pattern of domestic life. In the last century on Carriacou few households existed without having at least one or two men working at sea, on the schooners and sloops; the local economy provided barely sufficient food to sustain the island and hence men took to the waves, first to fish and haul and then later, to serve on steel vessels. Earlier, in the mid-Nineteenth century men began leaving home altogether, migrating first towards Trinidad and Aruba to work in cotton and also to the Venezuelan oil fields, then later to work on the building of the Panama Canal.

A hundred years later migration was towards London and Canada, and by the middle of the Twentieth century small reduplicated communities of Carriacouans began to cohere in Brooklyn, New York. Sometimes, young brides were brought from the island to these new societies, although that practice has nowadays ceased as women also migrate and control of the money supply on Carriacou is becoming less of a male affair as is the holding of land. Remittances and material supplies—*barrels* packed with gifts from these migrant workers—became an important staple for the island economy. By the Sixties, from a population of almost seven thousand souls, more than two hundred were leaving the island each year and the moneys which returned to the island from these *émigrés* greatly exceeded the total indigenous income.

Thus, since Eighteen Thirty-five, far more women have existed on the island than men—in the Nineteen Seventies the ratio was two to one, a fall from the mid-Nineteen Forties when it was four to one—and serial *liaisons* became conventional supplement to marriage practices: this was the custom of *friending* and of *keeping*, both of which involve informal rights and obligations. Kinship focussed not upon the nuclear family but on the maternal or co-uterine core of such groups, and it is said that *zami* or homoerotic relations between mothers—women whose men were absent, either at sea or in northern cities—were a common and accepted form of affinity.

In such situation—as recorded by Donald Hill in his late Twentieth century ethnography—due to this scarcity and frequent absence, men became transient partners and peripatetic between domiciles. Progenitors would sometimes, but not always, offer their women sums of money as recognition of affection that had been shared and was fruitful. Hence the identity of an individual in such social situations was organised with far more gravity given to the feminine side than to the genetically male side: to the mother, the sisters and aunts and the maternal brothers. It is out of this partially centripetal model of kinship that the individual Carriacouan psyche has developed, with the feminine core acting as primary locus in the generation of consciousness. It is the male partner who moves among households, unlike in other cultures—as, say the East Indian—where it is the new bride who moves to the patrilocal hearth. For instance, Canute Caliste, the much celebrated violinist and painter, had twenty-two children; three were with his married wife, and nineteen others were with eight different *friends*. Such a pattern is not atypical.

Without caste, class, or guild and trade association to organise the substance of self-conception, as occurs in other parts of the world, concepts of person on Carriacou are established bivalently: according to matriline, the mother's maiden name, the *blood* or 'relatives'; and according to the patriline, the name of the clan or the 'family'. The latter was typically endogamous, and the former, exogamous—marriage within the blood being unacceptable—and it was among the former grouping that prohibitions were found.

That is, the male marks what it meant to be exclusive, whilst the feminine is the sign of inclusiveness. Property inheritance typically lies within the agnatic male side rather than the uterine side, although this is changing, land being connected metonymically with what is sometimes called *ntoro*, an Ashanti word meaning spirit or semen: these being what were once called *nations*. There were originally nine of them, usually inherited through the father, which depended from tribal groups originally extant in west Africa: the Cromanti, who superceded Congo predominance after 1763, the Mandingo, Ibo or Igbo, and others. These compose what are still known as the nations.

Migration of all sorts has thus coloured life on Carriacou; the movement of human lives, of *flora* and food sources, and now of the money supply, has led to the constitution of a way of life that depends not upon its own place for survival and renewal but upon other and distant landscapes. Ironically, the former imperial *locale* has become the colony which endows wealth, for nowadays it is the case that remittances from overseas emigrants—from Manhattan and from London—maintain whatever kin groups have remained on Carriacou. No household is without an exile who works and occasionally visits and sometimes eventually returns to build a new and substantial concrete domicile. Inheritance has traditionally not been by primogeniture so land claims are often thoroughly complex, and in recent decades due to the foreign acquisition of land in order to build houses there has been an increasing commodification of terrain complicating this situation.

Thus there is a diminutive indigenous food production today as sufficient wealth exists to allow for imports: boats bring in goods from St. Vincent, Union, or Grenada. From a state of dearth there has come a certain degree of affluence, with at least one member of each native household returning with cash or sending annual cash disbursements, and the economy has assumed an artificial appearance having become dependent upon inflows of money rather than on internal and local production. It is not indigenous labour which presently drives the island economy. The former pedestrian and seafaring folk-culture is rapidly becoming a phenomenon of nostalgia or artifice and is simply relegated to the little Museum at Hillsborough as the isle becomes strangely cosmopolitan.

Today, in this new century, it is perhaps the funeral that takes priority in church rites, rather than marriage, and the interment of the dead and the subsequent *stone-feast* when a headstone is raised at the grave, is usually of greater significance than nuptial celebration or baptism. It is separation rather than union that receives such elevation, grief rather than joy. It is principally the non-migrant and senior members of the community, the *old heads*, who keep to a calendar of distant traditions or musical forms and festival observance; contemporary youth who have grown up with television, the internet, and cell-phones, and who have probably visited if not lived in New York or London, do not maintain the customs of the past, the dances and songs and folklore that sometimes reach all the way back to an African landscape and those anterior social affiliations.

During those early long years before the present, songs and stories, dances, melodies and musical rhythms, along with the Christian calendar, organised an essentially preliterate and almost non-monetary culture. Many of these mnemonic forms carried over from an African genesis into what have become the music, song competitions, and performances of today: the *maroons* which honour ancestors or *foreparents*, *parang*, originally a kind of serenade or satire music that came from Venezuela through Trinidad, and also the related and sinister tradition of the *job-job*. There was once calypso, then came reggae from

Jamaica and now there is rap: all these are old patterns of sound which express something memorable along with the lyric itself, sustaining an older folk culture into this new century's modernity.

Life today on Carriacou manifests a certain lightness and ease as work is no longer imperative for existence, whereas thirty years ago there was absolutely no surplus. As in much of the world however, where tradition has modernised within two or three decades, the former idyll—with its hard and laborious way of life—has been spoiled: for now music is not spontaneous and celebratory and dances are no longer festal. The electric guitar, reggae, and the steel drum, have replaced the Big Drum occasions, the Nation dances and the *quadrilles*. That earlier connection between the agricultural year and communal merriment no longer obtains and music and songs become similarly detached and ossify and perhaps become commercial; only a shell-like form is retained, often to be imitated without inspiration in an attempt to retrieve and revive a lost tradition.

When we first arrived on Carriacou we lived in an old house on the hillside at Craigston, to the south of the Hillsborough roadstead and near the hamlet of Bogles. The house had been built in a traditional West Indian style and was surrounded on three sides by a broadly roofed veranda where grackles and doves used to gather in the morning to receive a few crumbs. Once, all that land had been part of an estate owned by Mr. Edward Kent, the *last planter* in the Windward Isles, as he once referred to himself when I had visited him at his great house; Craigston had been the site of a three hundred acre cotton and then lime farm that had been initially established by the Scot John Urquhart some centuries ago; it had been in continual use until quite recently, being worked by old Mr. Kent. His establishment is still a beautiful aged building in lovely grounds situated on a hill overlooking the bay of Hillsborough. Hurricane Janet had wrecked the place but the structure was rebuilt upon its former Eighteenth century foundations and there remain many components of erstwhile plantation buildings, cisterns and several walls from former centuries.

Our old house had a high open roof with clerestory ventilation and a long enclosed passage at the rear for drying clothes and laundry, for when the rains came everything became damp and foul with humidity. The house was built with a large cement cistern as its foundation where rainwater from the tin roof was collected, and the building's axis was aligned with the trade wind for coolness. The windows were large and had only shutters and were without glass panes and the front wall of the house folded open to expose the interior. Inside, the rooms were decorated in tropical style with canvas and hardwood furniture and a few fine paintings by Canute Caliste and Eric Johnn. Curious pieces of coral decorated the bookshelves and large empty pink shells were used as containers. Old prints of Eighteenth century maps and picturesque Grenadine landscapes along with etchings of naval vessels were on the walls. The bedrooms were hung with gauzy white mosquito nets that occupied most of the interior space being suspended from high and timbered ceilings.

There were humming-birds and grassquits in the bougainvillea and hibiscus around the house and a few venerable iguanas; a citrus garden edged with coconut palm and tall banana plants surrounded the building. Below us was a small beach where pelicans constantly dived and where frigate birds were always gliding. Small bats circled us at dusk, squeaking in their ultrasonic way, as fireflies oozed tiny plosive flashes upon the indigo night in brief spots of tangerine fission. Sometimes small schools of tarpon would herd fish into the bay and systematically feed off the trapped schools for days, an image that delighted my younger son who would sit and watch the black fins arcing through the waves as the predators hunted.

Beyond the hillside was the abandoned lime factory with baobabs and armoured silk-cotton trees growing within rotten sandstone walls. Owls and kingfishers lived there among the manchineel trees and a few village boys would gather at dusk to bathe at a disused water tank beneath drooping casuarinas. Much of the old distillery equipment was still standing and appeared like beautiful and archaic sculptural forms. On the shore, north of the point on Sparrow Bay, was an overgrown cemetery which had partially fallen into the sea. The headstones were lopsided and green with mould and the names inscribed were all of one kind, for agnatic families had formerly each possessed their own interment grounds. These sites play an important role in the annual dry-season maroon festivals and at that site the MacKenzies and MacDonalds predominated. In the bay itself, within one of the collapsing sand-banks, my younger son unearthed what was an old neolithic burial site where the lime factory land bordered on the shore, and for a while our rooms were carefully littered with his collection of coarse ceramic sherds which he eventually donated to the Museum at Hillsborough; a building that had until not so long ago been a cotton ginning mill.

Over the years we returned each winter to that island, flying down to Grenada where we used to sometimes spend an evening wandering about the old naval port of St. George's with its stone godowns and piers and *carenage* and many commercial boats. Then, in the early morning, we would take the *Osprey*, a small fast ferry that was run by a Philippino family, across the bumpy channel—with its shark, dolphin, and flying-fish—to Carriacou.

In time we walked along every road, track, and path of the island, from Windward to St. Louis. On the airy and salutary coast about Bellevue we even tried to purchase our own house; property titles, due to the complexity of kinship, made any clear deed of ownership impossible however, and we abandoned the plan. Near the old lime factory at Dumfries—once the largest farm on the island—we discovered wonderful gentle pastures and often went there of an afternoon to lie in the grass and snooze or read under the red blossom of an old poinciana tree. Crossing over the ridge that demarcated the island, at the highest point on the way, about Belair, a view both east and west was possible: out towards the reefs and haze of the swelling Atlantic, and beyond our own lee shore, towards Jack Adan isle with its many terns and its strangely weird rock-formation of once-molten iron deposits, and further, towards the calmer cyanine-tinted Caribbean.

It was on Carriacou that I wrote part of a book called *Windward*. This was a work concerned with human love as a phenomenal metaphor and how amity presents the tissue of moral transition, the drama which coheres psyche into an individual expression or medium. I had begun by working on the idea of the *femme fatale*, a figure who—for me—best depicted the phenomenon of consciousness at its most pure and unaffected, without attribute or feature. On Carriacou, the feminine was for me conceptually far more nuanced and complex than the male, and its symmetrical response to the environment posed questions that were not complemented by the other sex.

In later years I had begun to work on another book called *Eros*. It was a book about naturalism, of landscape and animal life, particularly birds, and was an attempt to describe a balanced and equable place, in which the utopian harmonies of human and natural existence obtained. It was a depiction of paradise lost, in a sense, an exclusive synthesis or reconstruction of experience and literary form: a *georgic* world that was no longer found on earth but which had left sufficient traces for it to be reformulated by the imagination. In my eye that was a profoundly feminine rather than male organisation for its desire was reiterative rather than being inclined towards separation.

It is possible—only partially—to reclaim the places that once inhabited literature and to re-assemble that quality of human equanimity as it once existed in parity with nature. Such an ideal possesses a moral aspect, where abuse and cruelty are rare and where beauty is common. Is it not remarkable that most of the violence which occurs in the world today is performed by young men; the feminine usually has no part in such affairs, tending more to the physically pacific.

Carriacou, like so much of the world nowadays, possesses little that is forcefully indigenous. The migration of ideas and of persons, both systematically and randomly, has produced a contemporary culture which has long thrived upon concoction and the syncretic. Perhaps human life is intrinsically derived from the movement of bodies and ideas, and later, of goods or things that signify ideas. Human identity can be seen as federal in nature, composed of many divergent and differing elements that constellate only in terms of nomenclature or nominal apparence on certain brief and formal occasions. Consciousness will always move in search of acclaim and it is only in excessive inherence that it begins to become redundant and decay: the motive and agile being far more creative than the fixed. Yet it is the latter which will always seek to dominate, rather than to join and evolve.

Certain birds—like humming-birds—migrate gradually, the males preceding the females by a week, and the juveniles following on their maiden passage a week later. These latter birds who have only just learned how to fly must have been genetically encoded with an impulse and navigational programme, unless such information had been communicated to them in another fashion. Perhaps human beings also possess a rudimentary germ that continues to compel them to move about the earth and it is the profanely urban and sedentary which is profoundly artificial, inhibiting this natural effort. Nowadays, more than half the human population of the globe live in cities.

It is the ephemeral and the elusive, the inherently transient, which stamps us and marks us in time; out of time, literature takes us a bit further. Ultimately, our thought and emotion are founded upon an ability to perceive what we are not and our desire to emulate such conditions or properties. We are created according to affection and its obverse, domination, as much as by *locale*, and we evolve socially in relation to things and names being exchanged. So much vanishes in time—if not everything—except perhaps that ancient emotion of melancholy, of separation or grief, that which recollects a former love for something which in our various transports we have forsaken or lost. Only a vague and voluntary intimation remains perpetually as an affective or intellectual terrain upon which all our subsequent sensation and perception exists.

The isle, being just over six miles in longitudinal extent and up to two miles broad in part presents no serious difficulty for those going on foot; none of the ways are arduous or extreme and although unpaved in many places the tracks are generally easy because of their age. The ruins of Carriacou possess a naval or nautical Eighteenth century air as do early depictions of the place in drawings and prints. The isle is fragrant and beneficently delicious and the

Kayak people dignify their language and are generous in manner, proud of their nation and cultural inheritance. My wife had spent much of her girlhood on the nearbye and smaller Grenadine isle of Mustique and so our arrival and intermittent residence on Carriacou was, for her, very much a homecoming; what the Greeks refer to as *nostos*, as in the word 'nostalgia'.

During our later and more settled years we lived at *Grenan*, a small bungalow that was east African in design and fashion, on the western shore of the island between Craigston and the village of Bogles; it was just north of where we had initially dwelled. Bogles was famed for its smuggling and only a few years previously the island police had opened fire on a small vessel lying just off Sparrow beach because it had been about to offload contraband goods.

Our small ochre-painted dwelling had a red tiled roof and old fashioned monsoon shutters and its large bougainvillea bushes and thorny citrus and mandarin trees were frequented by shy mocking birds, grackles, and noisy vireos; little yellow bananaquits would often fly into the rooms and perch on the fans. There were many lizards and small umber-skinned boas would knot themselves upon the branches of the flamboyant trees. The physical plant of the lime factory was now in a state of general wreckage and during periods of drought the children from Bogles would visit its large cisterns for their water supplies and bathing needs. The boilers and vats looked like the modern sculpture of Anthony Caro and my wife took many startling photographs of those old forms and shapely volumes. Now, centipedes and bats were the only creatures to inhabit the degraded rooms of the factory and at night the cruel and bloodthirsty little manicou would patrol there. I used to have such vibrant and dramatic dreams at *Grenan* of a people whom I did not recognize, their dances and faces and the feathery clothing and head-apparel that they wore were so unlike anything that I understood. In fact such folk became almost familiars to me in those days and I knew them and their expressions and *personae* although the dreams were always silent.

Each winter the owner of a small restaurant at Bogles would set off fireworks at midnight on New Year's Eve and we would be woken up and would go outside onto the lawn beside the sea and watch the display as it sprayed above the shore and silvery breaking waves. The immense dancing multitude of stars would be up there in the heaven, complex and timeless. One December Venus was ascendant in the hours before dawn and rose above the ridge behind our house; she was then so bright as to actually cast a thin shadow during moonless hours, so gleaming with radiance and intensity as to throw an outline from our naked figures onto the grass.

In the wet months of the year rainbows shifted and circled about us in that little house and if we swam in the sea off Sparrow we would often find ourselves beneath the arc of such spectra as dark grey squalls of rain moved across the Caribbean waters and the swells would sometimes be up to twenty feet in height. To the north, Union Isle rose up out of the ocean, its pointed hills triangular and sharp. Many pelicans frequented our shore and would plunge into the waters about us as we swam; the sea there was empty for almost three thousand miles westward until the countries of Nicaragua and the Costa Rica. Once, I had risen before four one morning in order to sit at my desk—in those days I was working on an essay about the kinship and marriage systems of the Kayaks which, for historical and demographic reasons were unpredictably intricate—and outside, as I strolled the garden in the sweet night air, low in the west and settling towards the rocks of Jack Adan isle, a rouge and ponderous moon in full eclipse was visible, crimson and vast, hovering in the gentle inky silence.

One of our preferred walks was from *Grenan* up the hill towards Belair, where two British cannon still pointed out over the town and port of Hillsborough, all that remained of sixteen former batteries that had once been located around the coast. From that vantage we overlooked the settlement below with the grey outline of Grenada and its outlying isles to the south; behind us lay the tall bulk of High North, the most prominent point of Carriacou. There used to be a small *tortarium* up there next to the cannon, where several old tortoises lived out their years, and our children loved to watch those tediously slow creatures and to feed them cucumber. I frequently visited Belair of an evening in order to sit and gaze out over the island towards the southern and generally uninhabited promontory of St. Louis.

Sometimes I went swimming from that southern headland with two friends who had a solitary house on the hillside and their tree-covered dwelling would be just perceptible in the evening shadow. They were keen and competitive swimmers and we would go far from the shore into open water. In those years I would often swim for up to three hours a day, for swimming, like walking was an integral element in the Romantic tradition and its pursuit of a picturesque sublime and thus an important medium for my thought.

The gorgeous and cerise embroidered evening sun above Mont St. Louis would be setting and tall golden clouds would for some minutes bear the cosmic and magnificent aspect of another universe and life. Whatever the visual pleasure up there at Belair I never paused for long, hurrying downhill again in order to arrive at home before an unlit indigo darkness came upon the island. In some of the villages that I passed there would be a lighting of fires outside of cabins and folk would be resting on their verandas after a day of work, talking quietly as children and dogs played and small bats skipped through the black mosquito-perforated air.

My wife, being an ardent animal rights *activiste* would sometimes greet me on my return in the company of several four-foot iguanae that she had purchased and rescued from a hunter; our daughter was always delicately horrified by these prehistoric animals as they roamed the grounds and tried to climb the coco-palms. On another occasion I was met with the sight of two large and heavy hawksbill turtles which she, along with our naturalist friend Dario Sandrini, were taking down to the beach in order to liberate; the creatures having been purchased from fishermen who had found them tangled in their nets. For both Dario and my wife the companionship and the emotive loyalty shared with animals were a vital component in their emotional life and dogs, cats, owls and other birds, horses and donkeys, all these creatures participated in their world of amity just as much as human friends; such was their moral view of the affective universe.

Another of our favourite walks that we invariably accomplished on each visit to Carriacou occurred along the eastern side of the island: from an upland junction called Six Roads, south towards the hamlet of Bellevue, a distance of perhaps three miles. That way was along the Atlantic coast of the isle and possessed an outlook towards an offshore reef and distant rocks. The view was spectacular with the whiteness of breaking seas upon stony shelves beneath an immense tropical sky; it was like the savage austerity of the Lakonic coast in the eastern Peloponnese where I had walked far in my youth and I loved that image of strong inhuman beauty for its vigour and the distinct colours of aerial, ocean, and mineral formation.

We would wander all the way above those slopes, perhaps halting at the Cow Foot Inn if it was open, where a woman called Theresa—who had lived for many years in London—now served cold drinks and grilled food. Christine David, the Carriacou folklorist, lived at the hamlet of Belmont, which is where the way finally descended down into the sailing harbour of Tyrrel Bay, once the site of a grand plantation called Harvey Vale owned and run by James Bartlet in the late Eighteenth century. Nowadays the land on the down-side of the Bellevue road was uncultivated and barren having been over-utilised in the early Twentieth century for the cash-crop production of ground-nuts. During the walk we would pass one of the two defunct wells on that side of the island, presently in disuse and overgrown. The lack of forestation and the old stony pastures gave that region of Carriacou a wild and slightly Scottish aspect.

The road was a narrow unpaved track and had existed for several centuries since the Seventeen-hundreds when first the French and then the British took possession of the island from the few Caribs who inhabited it. In recent years the sparse little hardwood and shingled houses of that district had begun to disappear, either falling into abandonment as the inhabitants migrated away from the island to work in North America or England, or were knocked down and built over by affluent returning migrants who wanted larger and more substantial concrete dwellings and not something fabricated of mere teak and mahogany.

When our daughter was still an infant I would carry her on my back in a rucksack and we used to wander the island during sunny afternoons. My wife's best walk was up the hill from *Grenan* and over the ridge and down towards the village of Windward. The inhabitants there were of Scottish descent and were fair and many possessed Scots' names; the place was renowned for boatbuilding and its racing sloops were famous. Even now there were often one or two vessels being constructed upon the sands in the shade of mimosa trees and several boats would always be on anchor. Carriacou held a regatta each year in August and sailing vessels would come from all about the Antilles to compete in the round-island events.

The windward and Atlantic side of the isle was very different from our coast for there the trade winds were steady, strong, and salutary, whilst our side of the isle was more tropical in vegetation and insect-ridden. In the east a reef kept the ocean force away and further off were the small islands of Petit Martinique and Petit St. Vincent; the former being distinguished for its mariners and—until recently with the introduction of VAT—for the art of illegal trafficking. Looking down from the road at that prospect was always a wonderful moment and as one crossed over from one side of the isle to the other the transition was startling. A small graveyard was up there near to a pond where young brown cattle grazed, often with egrets upon their backs or about their hooves.

We used to amble down the hill and pause at one of the general stores where we would find something cool to drink, perhaps calling upon the village priest—Father McDonald—for an exchange of news, before we continued our route north-westward about the marine cemetery and the path leading down to the swampy mangrove shore of Petit Carenage where a shipwrecked coaster lay upon its beams surrounded by bleached and torn coral. We often stripped and swam in the turquoise foaming water of that beach and collected shells but we never remained long for the sand-fleas were voracious. The sheer island of Union was in the near distance with many boats anchored off its brilliant shore. Then our track bent southwards around Gun Point back towards our part of the coast, going through a cool shadiness of forest canopy where hundreds of lizards rustled unseen and just below Anse la Roche the bright macaws of the retired *thespian* Robert Cooper would perhaps screech and swoop with brash elation overhead.

Returning from that walk on one occasion—as we entered the vicinity of Bogles—there was a sound of drumming and of communal singing to be heard. Bogles was celebrated for its Rastafarian drummers but this was something different. As we entered the village proper a terrific solemnity was about the place and we soon realised that a funeral was occurring. For a second I wondered if the obsequies were for the eldest son of the family who kept the general store in the village, for he was with the British infantry in Afghanistan; but a passing acquaintance—the Methodist minister, Jack Russell—informed us that the memorial was for an old woman who had just expired, one of the *old heads*. The village matrons were all well dressed and wore hats and the men were in dark suits and white shirts; the drumming and sonorous monodic chanting came from inside a public building and we quickly deviated from the road and went away towards the shore, not wishing to intrude upon the service. Carriacou was profoundly Christian and yet ancestors and ancestral worship were essential to the practice and all the little family graveyards that dotted the isle were sites of much reverence and continual devotion; dances always began with rum libations offered to the familiar deceased.

One walk that I did which was not successful was upon the shoulder of High North, the most elevated peak of Carriacou, set at an altitude of just over three hundred metres. Wherever we walked on the island High North was always present as our witness and I would look up at it with uneasy frustration, often wondering if there was a route through its thorny scrub. I never realised that there was a path to the summit until last year when two friends told us about their ascent. That was a year of drought and the land was terrifically yellow and dry; cisterns were empty and ponds stale and water had to be shipped in from Grenada and sold or sometimes it was stolen from houses whose owners were absent. This meant that the path on High North was accessible and not beset by an overgrowth of cacti; our friends had shown us photographs taken from summit where a panorama of three hundred and sixty degrees was possible to the eye.

One afternoon I had been returning along the old Eighteenth century track from Windward following the northern circuit *via* Petit Carenage and Gun Point and had stopped at a friend's house at Honeyhill to inquire about this path. "Well, where the track turns ninety degrees to the left then ninety degrees to the right and above it there is a pasture," I was told, "at the top you might see the path."

I did this and began to ascend through much dense and low forestation, for a trodden corridor was barely visible and well overgrown. At the top of the ridge, slightly bewildered and very scratched I came upon a large meadow where I sat down on thick heavy grass and stared out onto sea and land. High North was to the left and still distant and I could find no further way to follow. Worse, I had lost my path and began to wander through unkempt forest, becoming torn and cut and bleeding. It was really a *mauvais quart d'heure* as the plants up there became suddenly strange and unearthly, unlike any other vegetation that I had seen on the isle. They reminded me of the kind of forestation that one finds in the lofty Rowenzori mountains in central Africa, possessing weird and unfamiliar forms, some of them being gigantic and almost consciously uncanny. It was also drizzling with rain that day and the air up there was misty and for half an hour or so I blundered about trying to regain my course, feeling horribly uneasy as I lost all sense of direction but that of descent. I did soon secure the way and made haste homeward, bloody and thirsty and feeling foolish for disregarding my friend's injunctions not to go up there at that time of the year and certainly not without a cutlass.

Walking in outlying areas can be extremely mystifying and confusing; potentially that was part of the experience, to lose all sense of order and emotional balance as one entered a state that could at times become dangerous. This had happened to me on several occasions long ago in Greece when I had been walking down in the south, far from roads or dwellings; then I had become completely disoriented, anxious, and almost deranged. That was one of the intrinsic qualities of real walking—if one was not vigilant and was carried away by the intoxication of the walk—the possibility of mental and emotional disorder could overcame the pedestrian. Thereafter, wherever we walked on Carriacou the perpetual appearance of High North always left me with a sense of haughty defeat which was mildly intolerable; as yet, I have never found the time to attempt another ascent, which is similarly disagreeable.

On another occasion I set off alone in an early afternoon towards Windward but by a long route, initially heading south, turning northward only when I was past Six Roads. My family were busy doing something else that day, perhaps they were on a boat somewhere.

A true walk is always slightly disturbing—perhaps in something like a sacramental fashion—in the sense that the walker enters into an altered state. That afternoon as I began on my venture I had been excited to be at last taking this one trail on the isle which we had not yet explored. On that day however, at the outset I was not sufficiently impassive nor mentally prepared to walk and was dilatory and idle-minded and consequently had been attacked by two dogs. I had beaten off one of the animals but the other had almost managed to corner me against a spiky hedge before its master appeared and saved my skin. I always made a point of walking with a good cane, but on that afternoon I had left home hastily and without a stick as my daughter had been playing with it and mislaid it. In India I actually carried a steel swordstick against dogs and other large quadrupeds although only once had I needed to use it and that had been in folly.

Then the mini-bus which I had taken to the Six Roads junction had deviated far to the south and left me on the road between L'Esterre and Harvey Vale, more than a mile away from where I wanted to be. So the commencement to this walk had truly gone awry in several ways for my mind had not been rightly engaged with the project. Walking, for me, was never a casual nor lackadaisical affair, not if one was to achieve any conversion from the experience, where vision would exceed the mundane and ordinarily diurnal.

So it was a while before my psyche was actually with me and I finally settled to a pace and its singularity and managed to focus my attention properly on the walk. I descended the long straight track down towards what had once been the biggest plantation on the island at a place called Dumfries, formerly an estate of more than five hundred acres that had been run by Mr. William Tod. The last planter to farm there had been our neighbour Mr. Kent and his rotting obsolescent machinery and buildings were still visible through the trees and underbrush. Now only small brown cattle browsed the pastures where once lime and citrus had been cultivated. At some point there must have been a dead cow among the forest for the stench was terrible and I actually ran for a while in order to escape the violently noxious odour.

On that coast just to the north of Dumfries at Sabazan an American archaeological team had six years ago excavated and discovered large-scale Arawak camps dating back to the end of the first millennium of the Common Era. In fact this had been one of the best archaeological find-sites in the West Indies and artifacts from there were now on display in the Museum at Hillsborough: beautiful ceramic and shell objects of adornment, clay figurines, and nicely decorated pottery, along with strange conical forms called *zemis*, which were of unknown ritual utility.

The eastern side of the island was in the shadow of the post meridian sun and was cool and breezy and many of the trees on the windward side of the track were bent into a form emulating the Trades. Frigate birds and terns were floating above the sea and in that part of the isle there were martins shooting about the air. Once or twice I noticed a heron as it silently glided away from my approach. The way was rough but passable and like the other coastal routes on Carriacou was originally established in the Eighteenth century; now and then I would pass some straying goats or disturb a few diminutive donkeys who were resting in the shade. Dragonflies were in the air and the vegetation was noisy with lizard and iguana, large hermit crabs scuttled on the ground and thick black millipedes were in busy profusion. Pigeons were loud with their wing-beat and doves fluttered about the branches of mahoe and poui trees.

The path soon rose and ran along the top of cliffs. White Island and Salines were to the south, strongly silhouetted in the hazy light and delineated by a stark white fringe of surf about their base. The perspectives were giant and remarkably distinct and visually satisfying: the contrast of ocean and sky and high cloud formation all contributed to a transcendentally precise scene. Such was the virginity of the picture that I could feel all sense of myself disappearing in the extraordinary natural harmony which excluded any indication of humanity, for in moments of real solitude one is never alone but is simply assimilated into the physical virtue of things. I walked and walked, halting now and then to rest in a pasture or to examine a ruined cistern or some fallen walls or a shallow bridge across a ravine. The walk was exhilarating and rejuvenating, such was the majestic acumen of light and the purity of the topography which still retained an aspect of old centuries and pastoral time. Up to my left on the far hillside was the forest and to my right the Atlantic ocean glittered and seethed and it was as if my spirit had been restored to an amazing and supernatural world where suffering and resentful humanity did not exist.

Passing the ruins of the old Kendeace estate of Mr. Robertson, the track curved in towards the next concavity of coast, that of Grand Bay where David Mill had once cultivated the land. It was not so long ago in living memory on Carriacou that people inhabited dwellings fabricated of clay and wattle with thatched rooves, but now all that presently remained of former time were a few brown sandstone foundations and carious broken tanks. Soon, my attention was drawn by what appeared to be an ancient midden, where piles of desiccated and decayed conch shells were heaped upon the sands; by then the way was level with the sea and ran closely parallel to the waterline. I walked through an area of sea-grape in order to inspect the place and found mounds of shells and animal bones.

Further on, the basalt sand was littered with thousands of sherds, Arawak pieces, some of which I picked up, either for their lovely molding or their painted decoration, and I found some damaged stone instruments, probably pestles. I could not believe the proliferation of so much disjecta—amongst the mangrove roots and crabs and driftwood—and where the sand fell away in a small cliff-face into the sea one could actually view the various temporal levels of refuse. The recent heavy rains must have washed away the earth and uncovered the material. The Arawaks had been destroyed by the Caribs who, in turn, had been cruelly displaced by the Europeans, such was the predation of those many centuries. It was only the shrubs and trees, introduced from far away on the other side of the planet, which had discovered harmony and equation on the isle.

Not much longer after this I began to enter an area of casuarinas and manchineel and down by the water's edge I could see dozens of grave-stones. Some of them were awash in the ocean and lopsided and melancholic in appearance, marking the mutability and impermanence of human monuments; even death could not be commemorated beyond a few years. The Drummonds, the Cloudens, the Coys, and the Quashies were all there, the headstones dating back to the early Nineteenth century. One memorial, which was set away from the others and had perhaps been a crypt which had collapsed, bore a fine inscription to Hugh Munro who had passed away in Seventeen Seventy-eight at the age of forty-nine years. He had been the planter who had farmed the Limlair estate of over three hundred acres.

Soon I re-entered the habited world and my lone tranquility and inwardness began to retreat. Banana, papaya, and gouava were cultivated in patches outside of singular households among plots of bean plants and here and there a Norfolk pine grew upwards and laundry and goats and metal implements were strewn about the ground. There was a paucity of material wealth thereabouts and I felt that this area of Carriacou—without a metalled road connecting it to the rest of the isle—was lost and slightly disengaged from the Twenty-first century. Mosquitoes and fleas began to bite me as I walked. Most of the houses possessed black plastic cylindrical containers which were cheaper to install than the earlier kind of roofed stone cisterns. For a while I was accompanied by an old lady who wore a cotton frock and felt halt and we chatted although I could not comprehend a word of her toothless *patois*; all that I realised was that she was going to the bakery.

I passed the big green pond at Dover where some boys were playing with a toy boat and made my way along the road towards Windward where I drank a luxurious bottle of water. Then I turned uphill and set off back towards Bogles and home, happily tired by the day's progress and my pedestrian visions.

Rarely on a good walk did I not—for a tentative few minutes at least—experience the passing emotion of grief. Grief is perhaps more intrinsic to the human condition than even the knowledge supplied by affection, for the latter is—in its founding—physiological in nature and touching upon the beveled rims of sensation. Whereas grief and the comprehension of loss are phenomena that are thoroughly historical, born of experience rather than of anatomy. It was for all those temporary instants during my peregrinations when I had looked upon the terrestrial beauty of landscapes that I grieved, for if a walk is both good and true it will connect at some point metonymically with all of one's previous exceptional walks.

A walk, if it is successful, becomes a brief receptacle of beauty and those images form a nucleus in our memory; for natural beauty—as a perception—is only and always ephemeral and can only either be momentarily experienced or for a second retrieved. Thus during the early stages of my Windward walk for a few minutes I felt all those other great walks returning to me as I reconnected to their sequence; sojourns that had transformed me each in an individual fashion by virtue of their apprehension of terrestrial beauty. Also, being alone and peregrine I remembered those wonderful friends with whom I had once strolled and conversed; companions who were either now deceased or far removed in time and whose association and fondness were lost.

For beauty is necessarily spontaneous and transitory, that is perhaps the uniquely profounding principle of beauty, that it is perpetually transient. Even the beauty of a piece of music or of a painting or an object of architecture like the Parthenon in Athens is necessarily ephemeral; for the experience is always of momentary duration and the sensibility does not remain. Beauty cannot be recalled nor remembered, only the fact that one *did* experience such visual, audial, or plastic harmony can be sometimes regained. Perhaps there exists a trace of that impulse towards transformation, some cell within us is effected and beauty does modify us during those instants: there is some exchange and beauty actually is causative or efficacious and not simply ephemeral after all, and there does exist a residual ideal which can renovate our standing in the world. By definition, walking is transient and peripatetic and the experience is momentary and completely impermanent; one is only moving across the surface of a landscape and to become stationary is to terminate the walk.

On that afternoon as I went along the steep windward coast of Carriacou I was suddenly reminded of several of my previous wonderful saunterings and for a few minutes I felt an indelible sadness for the loss of those truly immaterial and insubstantial experiences of beauty or amity. Now, I could simply only recall that such moments *had* occurred, that is, I could recall the sequent emotions that signified those original experiences, for the latter could not possibly be re-possessed: the experience and possibility of renewing or repeating those experiences no longer existed and they were lost.

There was the ancient way along the south-east flank of the Peloponnisos, below the late-Mycenaean citadel at Zarax with its titanic grey monolithic walls: a narrow course of hot dust that ran through olive and fig groves towards the Byzantine town of Monembasia. There were the purple and magenta hills of the Scottish isle of Lewis where I had once gone with my father-in-law in pursuit of woodcock, one early winter in the company of an old red pointer hound; the delicate outline of the Shiants were in the distance on a gunmetal sea, golden eagles were circling about us in the hills and now and then a shy solitaire stag could be spotted in the highland. I had walked long hours with my wife in American Maine, far up in the north-east along a promontory that reached down into the Bay of Fundy, where the rocks and stones and trees were archaic and almost paleolithic. In western Gujarat I had walked across a small saline desert one year, and boar and jackal had howled about our fire at night and at dusk tens of thousands of migratory Siberian cranes had come down to feed upon the winter grasses.

Beauty does not remain with us but perhaps it does change us. On a good walk I am always—at some point—reminded of those sole and enduring minutes when suddenly the *kosmos* and its being was open and its invisible and weightless pattern was available for viewing; before it quickly vanished leaving us with no recollection but only a bare memory that something perfect had been artlessly exposed. Such instants can never be repeated and one might only attempt the pursuit again in other and different situations. Companionship allows one to sometimes retrieve those cursory minutes when, in conversation we recollect such transient occasions which had once been shared and mutually enjoyed.

High North was invariably there, an impersonal spectator whom the world did not know, watching our small passages and endeavours. It was completely unaware of our traffic and ambitions, our insistence and inquisitiveness. It always remained a sign for me of that which was simple yet fully inaccessible; perpetually immediate and yet forever removed, exclusively observant of another *tempo* and perhaps absolute condition that was never to be actually experienced.

Like Odysseus, at the outset of our journey we are called Noman, and in order to travel onward we become expert in telling the enigmatic lies that formulate whom we think we are and how we might best be received. Speech is ultimately home, and the poets and those who sing or can recall the dances are the ones to perfect such places, always going to windward in search of another seamark.

~ On Friendship ~

III ~ II

ONE January morning when the air was still cold from a heatless night I set out for the little hamlet of Dhordo situated on the Indian margin of the Great Rann of Kacch in western Gujarat; to the north lay the border and hills of Pakisthan and far to the south lay the Arabian Sea. My intention was to walk across the small Banni desert towards the Chari Dhand, a seasonal marsh that lay about forty kilometres to the south. The *pani*, as it was called locally, 'the water', attracted many tens of thousands of migratory birds during the cool winter months and they came in great flights and skeins from Iran and Iraq and even from as far away as Siberia.

I had visited the arid and saline Banni on many previous occasions but these had always been during hot summery months when the mercury in a thermometer stood at about one hundred and twenty degrees *fahrenheit*; it was not possible to stay there for more than a few hours before becoming intoxicated by the heat and strong light. I had also often skirted part of the terrain in a vehicle but that kind of travel only leaves one with a cursory sense of a landscape and its animals, trees, and human inhabitants.

Earlier that day I had left my household and family at our house in Bidhada, a town in the south near the coast, and went up to Dhordo; I spent the night there at the home of Abdul who was the headman of the village and the friend of a friend. After I had arrived and we had gone to the privacy of his farmhouse we spent much of the later afternoon looking at videos of his horses—for he bred ponies for racing and trotting and also for dancing—which had been filmed across the border in Sindh where his brother competed the animals in fairs. He showed me many items of tack, carefully woven of coloured wools and impressed with silver, and we wandered about the farm calling for his dogs, to whom I was introduced. His ponies fetched huge prices at *melas*, the fairs, and were famous. Before evening came Abdul escorted me about the passages and courtyards and rooves of his many houses—for he had eight married offspring—introducing me to his kin. The buildings were of differing and non-uniform character, made of brick, concrete, mud, with either grass thatching or tiles, and were all of one contiguous architecture.

That night after dinner we sat up late in the guest-room with its family and ancestral pictures circling the walls, as Abdul played a *changu*, the Sindhi mouth-harp, one of the oldest of human musical instruments, and his nephew Mazhar played a harmonium and sang *ghazals* from the Mughal poetry of Ghalib, a favourite of mine as well. The mildness and endurance of their lives out there on the rim of the Rann and on the camber of the desert and the slowness which inhabited their seasons filled me with a strange awe and a sense that I was crude and unworthy. Their knowledge and understanding of that natural world and its bare life, their love for children, their constant reiteration of prayer throughout the day: these set the Banni people apart from the rest of the Kacch and I felt honoured to be so accepted with such warm facility, to receive so much open benevolence and amity that evening. For me, human kindness is the only and ultimate token of spiritual generosity.

The following morning I woke in the chilly blackness to the call of *muezzin*, a young and very beautiful voice, summoning the faithful to *namaz*; the little mosque was next door. Abdul quietly slipped out whilst I lay for a while beneath my quilt, and when he returned through the room he gave me a shake. I bathed and a shadowy figure brought in a dish of tea and I dressed and in not many minutes we were driving down a track to where Abdul quickly made his farewell and departed. He left me with Sujaval, one of his kin who was to be my guide and companion for the next couple of days.

Almost before Abdul had disappeared, Sujaval was off at what seemed a run, such was the velocity of his pace. It was like the start of a race and I had difficulty keeping up with him as we penetrated into dense thornwood forestation and followed a slim track in the sand. A blonde-coloured waning moon was to our left, low in the east, and all was silent and bleak, the sky a thin wash of grey. Soon Sujaval slowed his steps and we settled to a fast walk, moving between the spiky *prosopis juliflora* vegetation. There was no sound apart from our footfall and a mild susurration of frigid air as it passed through the cover. We walked like that for about an hour until the horizon began to become topaz and as sparse cornelian and turquoise birds began to flit about our way. We glanced at each other and smiled and that was the commencement of our walk.

Sujaval moved with a quick and short gait, with a measure that was exactingly repetitive and precise, almost mechanical. The Rabari—the herding community who lived to the south of Banni, men whom I had briefly walked with on my various saunters about the Kacch—proceeded with a much lengthier and loping pace, swaying their torso and shoulders as they stepped. I liked to walk with a long and more upright and swinging tempo, using my cane as a balance. It always amazed me how differently pedestrians went and how their bodies engaged so variously with such a simple human act.

My pace became automatic as if the earth were moving beneath us and unrolling, as the stars receded and more pipits began to flutter and dash about the coverts; it was still cold and I kept on pulling my head-dress, my *paghadi*, down over my ears. Occasionally there was a rustling of a small quadruped in the bushes and the sand was covered with their tracks which in the half-light I could not quite distinguish. I was also beginning to feel faint from the lack of sustenance that morning and from our haste, and only for a short while was I able to resist asking Sujaval to pause a minute whilst I took some bananas from my rucksack. He did not want to halt at all and just kept on walking for we had far to go. Before long I simply stopped and unslung my bag and removed the damp and battered fruit and offered him half of them and a packet of sweet Tiger Biscuits; then we sat and quietly ate.

Soon we were off again as the sun rose, tinted pink and tangerine. At that time of the year there is often a heavy dew in the Kacch during the last hours of pre-dawn and that is the coldest time of the night. As we set off again, the dew, visible as a dense white filmy saturation almost like ectoplasm, hung unevenly upon the land. For another hour the air remained tepid but then the day finally began to heat up with the upheaval of the sun.

We continued all morning, pausing now and then, once taking a few minutes of rest to drink some tea that Sujaval had brought in a plastic flask. The carefulness and precision with which he cleaned the steel cups and repacked his bag were impressive: there was an unhurried gravity about him and an exactitude that left me feeling uncouth and ill-mannered. As for his personal appearance, that was remarkable and visually stunning: here was no simple figure. Sujaval's hair and beard were stained a bright mandarin orange with henna; his wife must have done this recently for the colour was so pure and shocking. His skin was a dark umber brown, thick and pigmented by a life in the desert. He wore a bright turquoise *kurta* and baggy trousers, *choyani*, his head-dress was scarlet and white and his shawl—his *ajrak*, a dyed and block-printed cloth and perhaps the most valuable possession of a *maldhari* herder—was pale blue and crimson; the water bottle that he carried slung from the end of his stick was covered in a wooly cloth of broad red and white stripes. The stick was old and stained and heavy and thickly bound with iron wire to give it weight; he wore shiny black rubber-moulded footwear. This was not a man of reservations. Sometimes he would take an eroded pair of spectacles from his bag in order to look around and confirm our location.

All morning we walked, swinging along, following tracks in the powdery white sand. Often we were surrounded by *ganda-bhava*, the thornwood plant that had been taking over the Banni during the last thirty years, but usually we were in the open. There were many jackal tracks, big paw marks upon the ground, as well as those of boar and of *nilgai*, the blue buck; and now and then there were the asymmetrical curvy marks which a cobra had left. *Nag*, Sujaval would say bitterly, pointing with his stick.

The sun glared and the alkaline dust shot back a blue intangible light and I was soon longing for the delicious cool of dusk. A strong south-westerly was blowing off the sea forty or so miles below us, where the dhows would be coming in from the Iraqi Gulf and the fishing boats tacking out into the glittering aquamarine tide of Mandvi port. As the leonine sun moved towards zenith the sky lost its faint cerulean hue and became increasingly the colour of winter sapphire. I repeatedly took off my *paghadi* and retied it, making sure that it covered as much of my head as possible. With the steady and relentless buffeting of the wind and the sand in one's ears, it was not possible to hear well and I felt uncomfortably deafened by a small intense noise like a *tinnitus* which was not an agreeable sensation and left me feeling light-headed and occasionally vertiginous. I constantly heard voices, sounds of birds or bells that were almost fugitive yet remained indistinct, which was exasperating and disconcerting. Sujaval was steadily hawking and spitting as he smoked little *bidi* cigarettes and my nose and mouth were coated with superficial particles of dust causing me to contribute my own throaty growls.

There were many raptors—kites, tawny eagles, laggar falcons and buzzards, kestrels—in the air about us, some of them large and slow; beautiful birds that glided about, completely disregarding our presence as they soared away or perched upon branches of *piloo*. The happiness of the hundreds of birds, bee-catchers, swallows, and junkos, most of them migratory, was blissful and carefree, as it always is when there are no humans in the vicinity. Now and then we came across a few stray but hobbled camels, all of them with finely decorated brands upon their coats, of circles and dashes and zig-zags, and often wearing bead necklaces; their raucous groans and the occasional bass tinkle of their bells was a lovely sound. Sometimes we passed a few buffalo who were leisurely and ponderously grazing upon dry grasses, perhaps in the company of a boy-herder and occasionally a herd of zebu cattle ambled by in the opposite direction to us, their tall vertical horns and shining grey skins giving them the air of strange and archaic nobility.

Banni is said to have once been the largest grassland in Asia and with the annual monsoon it would become a green jewel of many and various grasses that were three or four feet in height. Thousands of pounds of *ghee* or clarified butter were once weekly exported south to the Kacchi capital of Bhuj, but those days were long gone. Although, with modern bore-wells and submersible pumps some villages like Dhordo still produce hundreds of litres of buffalo milk a day: so Abdul had proudly claimed that afternoon as we drove back from his farm and went to inspect his ponds and tanks. Breeding has now given way to only grazing, and the old patterns of migration northward during the dry season are precluded due to Partition and the frontier. Nowadays, the Banni was an eight thousand square kilometer *rakhal,* or seasonal savanna where ten thousand people lived and where about fifty thousand cattle existed; although scanty and erratic monsoons often decimated those herds.

The construction of dams in the Sixties to the south of Banni had stemmed the flow of waters into the little desert and the seasonal leaching of salt from the sand, and those prosperous grassy days were no longer extant. Zealous over-grazing as well as the invasive and voracious *prosopis juliflora* which destroyed all indigenous plants, had brought a harsh clime to the Banni. Several years of depredation by Rajasthani charcoal-burners had also denuded much of the landscape but that had fortunately now been made illegal and outlaw. Mining corporations were keen to exploit the enormous mineral deposits of the region and already several gigantic factories had been planted on its fringes; they of course also drained off water supplies and contributed to the rapidly declining water-table as well as wrecking the atmosphere. Many of the forty-plus villages were not affluent like Dhordo and subsisted in great impoverishment; my wife and I had sometimes visited those hamlets during our peregrinations and it was always a sad experience. Like most of the Kacch, the Banni was not well placed in terms of ruthless modernity and the traditional life and concord of centuries if not millennia was in serious jeopardy and the prey of calculating industrialists. Already wolves were almost extinct, and much other life, animal and human, existed only on the verge of a terrific instability.

Kacch possessed an ancient topography; it was once submerged beneath what is now the Arabian Sea, and fossils and petrified trees plus many kinds of once viable detritus from the Jurassic age still lie scattered and unmoved upon the earth. A physician friend from the port of Mandvi had once travelled with me up towards the Rann and taken me to a desolate but beautiful spot where he had located the remains of fossilised trees which were of that era, fifty or sixty million years in age. He himself had discovered dinosaur eggs in that same region which he kept in his private museum, a *cabinet* of natural treasures in a special room atop his house. As a physician he had been able to x-ray them and to see the foetal and mineralised creature within the shell.

The Indus Valley civilisation had flourished in these parts and the sophisticated ruined city of Dholavira lay just to the north-east of us. In those days the Indus flowed into the region before seismic change had shifted its flow, and I possess an early English map of the Kacch, designed and printed two hundred years ago, indicating the area of the Chari Dhand—where Sujaval and I were headed—as an inland bay and joined by Indus waters to the sea. The village of what is now Chari, where there are many traces of earlier habitation, was formerly a sea-port, as late neolithic Dholavira had also been. Such were a few of the transitions which time had effected in that region.

As we walked that day a sweetness and lyrical splendour hung about the utterly flat landscape and the gentle curvature of the earth was just perceptible. Large burnished doves occasionally fluttered about us as did a hoopoe and many stonechats and babblers. That linear flatness was perhaps, for me, the most compelling visual sign of Banni: an emptiness delineated simply by this horizontal mark which distinguished the bareness of blue sky from the soft dun-coloured dryness of sandy earth; there was no perspective to this potent visual field. The colours were almost Scottish—the hues and tones of the isles, but without the purples and crimson—such were the subtle visual qualities of the situation. The only unpleasance was the noise of the wind and the dust in one's ears that caused me to hear sounds which I knew did not exist and yet were nevertheless eerily maddening.

~ ON FRIENDSHIP ~

Some days previous, when I had driven up towards Dhordo, the dust storms had been terrific and visibility was between one and two hundred yards. At Dhrang, a temple precinct where my driver and I had halted for water and something to eat, the place was desolate and deserted: at the *dharmsala*, the hostel and its adjacent buildings, everything was locked and there were only a few people trying—in the dusty wind—to set up tents and gigs for the *mela* that was to happen in a week. Jagdish, my driver, went to a gate which was locked and banged hard on the wood. The door flew open with a clatter and we entered and it was quickly bolted against the wind. Inside was another world of vivid electric light, with Ahir women in their bright gaily embroidered clothes, and children scampering about tables lining the walls where meals were being taken. I felt that we had come in out of the snowy steppe, such was the quick passage from sterility and inimical harshness to this genial scene of laughter and human warmth.

That day as Sujaval and I walked was clear, the ingenuous wind no longer blew with such vigour and only swirled in small spinning tornadoes, ghostly dancing figures that moved slowly about us as if inspecting our presence. At one point, out of the shimmering open distance where the quartz light trembled and quivered, a herd of about an hundred camels appeared and crossed our path, accompanied by one man. He was a *maldhari* of the Phakirani Jath people who centuries before had migrated down from Iran. Not far away and to the north the gleaming saline diamond of the Rann sent up a deliquescent and flaring intensity into the sky, a ferocious glare that reflected down again upon miles of barren and sterile salt deposits: it was a whiteness of death out there, of Yama, a luminosity of no substance nor sign, something like I imagined the Arctic to be.

The emptiness dominated our mood and we rarely spoke, although, with my simple Gujarati and Sujaval's Kacchi—a dialect of Sindhi—we did not communicate much except to joke wordlessly about things; as most of human speech is merely *phatic*, a social and creative device and not actually communicative of information, this reticence did not really matter. *Sujaval*, I soon learned, was the name of a village in Pakisthan whence his family derived; it was a toponym and not a Quranic proper name.

For myself, to walk is to be in pursuit of the experience of beauty. That day, walking the miles upon a fine yielding sand as the sun arched over us and threw our shadows around us upon the earth, my mind gently settled to the *tempo* of our step and the sound of our feet upon the dust; as sand-grouse scattered around us and the stirring of small *animae* was occasionally audible.

It is difficult if not impossible to conceive of emptiness for human consciousness evades such an idea or perception, it cannot accept the perfectly candid and blank. The meaningless clarity of the Banni atmosphere became stupefying after a while and the horizon which encircled us completely was the only distinction to meet the eye. Even that was illusory, as the circle which held us was not fully perceptible and only completely existed in the imagination: for one could glimpse the annulation partially and never wholly nor simultaneously. There was never a complete line, for optically a straight edge was all that existed and only the sum of the several instances of curve supplied the conceptual illusion of circularity or hemisphere. Similarly, human life as a totality is only a project of mind, and as everyone knows, cognition is a great deceiver: we assume time and memory and translation but all that we actually possess is our present and that itself is constantly being superceded. We also possess a modicum of anticipation derived from such experience, but that too lacks material or authentic foundation. In all this variant experience it is amity which supplies us with our only true gravity.

Similarly the perception of open space is impossible without perspective, for we are not able to apprehend an absence of dimension and our psyche delivers the actual form. This is not the *picturesque* but the sublime, an indication of larger and supernal consciousness that is at times inherent to *locale*. Hence, for the mental traveller as pedestrian, visual beauty is more available, more accessible to his or her view than linguistic beauty which is naturally limited by its verbal or acoustic metaphors. Metaphor only refers to further metaphor until one is freed of such signification, whereas visual beauty is typically implied *via* the rules of composition and perspective, and, in the case of this particular walk that I was then performing, by the superb absence of such principles.

For me, walking is perhaps one of the most essential qualities of the human psyche and to be pedestrian is one of the most profound aspects of human awareness; in walking we become recipient of those terrestrial energies that once initially stamped our being with its primary images and emotions. If human culture is fundamentally allegory and if the human spirit itself is but metaphor—presented with a supersensible or non-inferential truth—then during the activity of walking, and I mean in an unpopulated and solitary terrain, those social or artificial aspects of consciousness are able to dissolve and dissipate and we might reclaim our initial sensibility for life on earth: that presently lost or forsaken condition of friendship with the natural world. If the aim of the walker is true, then walking can be considered a spiritual exercise.

Originally I had intended to cross the Banni alone and without a guide but my friends were all horrified at this and I had sagely changed my plans and sought out Abdul. I had wanted to walk during the full-moon nights of January, but a few days of malarial and brain-deadening fever back home at Bidhada had made that impossible. So I carefully plotted a compass route using my maps—though none of the maps of the area were accurate nor meticulous—and I had chosen a north-south direction: for on one side of the Dhand lay a hill and on the other a small mountain, which would supply me with bearings. The real problem was not the distance but the nature of the ground itself: what would the conditions of the sand be like and how much ground cover was there, both of which might not allow me to keep a straight course. Thus I could not estimate the time required even though the distance by my reckoning was only about forty kilometres to the Dhand and another fifteen to Foulay where the road began again; hence the crucial importance of moonlight in case I had to walk after the sun had gone below the horizon. I did not want to be out there in an entire darkness with wolves and caracal and boar about, and certainly, to sleep out there in the blackness without a fire was not a good prospect, for not only were there the cobras—which everyone dreaded—but there were scorpions, and not simply one kind but four varieties.

So when I missed the moon I became anxious about the walk and very glad when Abdul suggested, in fact he insisted, that I join with Sujaval. Little did I know what a great treasure that man would be for me, and how simple diurnal amity in a natural setting was to become such a source of compassionate riches and wisdom.

Once or twice we paused in the thin shadow of *prosopis juliflora* and ate a few more biscuits. The shape of Dhinodar appeared before us at about noon, dry and volcanic in silhouette; that was satisfying and I ceased to constantly check my compass course of two-forty degrees. Kyro, our other way-point, appeared to the right much later, conical and dark. Our destination lay precisely midway between those two marks.

I was amazed by the intricate and yet powerful beauty of the day, it was overwhelming in its solitude and unaffected form. Such beauty cannot be transmitted and is only ever immediate and cannot be translated for it excludes all other experience and remains only in place, unable to continue beyond its moment. I was crucially and poignantly aware of how much I was then receiving and how quickly it would vanish. Sujaval, in his silent and dignified way, had spent most of his life out there in that absolute transience, and when we halted for *namaz* he would throw down his bag and go and wash hands and feet and returning, would cast his *ajrak* upon the earth and falling down upon his knees he prayed. I was in awe of such virtue and unqualified devotion: aniconic monotheism was the only act possible for the believing heart in such a territory and I quickly realised how hypothetical in fact life was out there without that experience of unoccluded prayer.

In such land where the munias and buntings flitted about carelessly and larks rose up at our passing, where the vacance of furtive light and heated air encapsulated us with a candid solution of quietness, it was impossible not to perceive and become joined with a spirit of place and for all sense of person to evapourate; such was the stability of those untimed hours and their invisible movement. In that situation one's psyche could amplify itself, no longer being distinct from its environs. The realisation of beauty is perhaps that apperception of our true being, and between illusion and emptiness lies the experience—not as a state nor as a practice nor even as a category—as a condition which is soundless and possessing no position nor status, being immaterial yet forceful. Such became my sensibility of walking that day.

At one point during the afternoon we came across a *maldhari* encampment, a small circle of cut and piled thorn-hedge that protected a family and their juvenile camels from predation during darkness. Whilst the animals grazed upon the bronze-coloured vegetation various members of the family performed tasks or merely sat in a shadow and observed. The women in their russet dyed cloths and heavily complex nose-rings and numerous ivory bangles were wonderfully attractive and modest, veiling themselves at our approach. Their gorgeous cloths were stained a profoundly maroon-umber saturation of pigment and were magnificent; they went about the camp performing the milking, carrying full pots balanced upon their heads.

We went and sat with a herder and hardly spoke, just maintaining a solemn reticence. After a while, Sujaval handed over his steel can and the man gave it to a boy to take and fill. The Phakirani eschew almost all acquisition of property and are thoroughly devout in their practice of prayer and nomadism. For them, constant physical movement, along with their herds of camel, is an act that emulates the first pilgrimage of the Prophet. Their diet is mainly camel milk— also our diet for the next two days—and they refuse to sell it but only give it away if required or if they possess a surplus. When the Chari Dhand dries up during the hot season they set off with their herds towards the west to the desolate and unpopulated area about Lakhpat where they lived in small and very lovely reed cabins. I had recently been up there and had given one family whom I knew some photographs that my wife had taken in the previous year. Their joy and amazement at receiving the prints actually made me feel foolish, such was their unpretentious and unmixed happiness.

Now and then we passed other *maldhari* but without any exchange of word or even a glance. The silence of these people shocked me, for it was unlike what I knew of similar folk in the eastern Mediterranean who were always effusive. At one point two men passed on a small motor-cycle, a Honda-Hero, and then halted. Taking out a cell-phone, one of the men turned up the volume and the sound of *muezzin* calling the office of prayer was audible across the sand. Both men went down on their knees and facing west began to formally rinse their hands with sand as a gesture of ritual cleanliness before bending their heads to the earth in devout submission.

As the great sun arched downwards we began to approach the Dhand; often would we disturb groups of crane that were browsing upon the earth, and they would rise upon their huge grey wings, croaking as they moved away from our course. Flocks of teal and pochard were visible low in the air, and now and then herons and egrets would pass overhead. Suddenly hundreds of camels seemed to be gathering around us as they were being driven down to the water by boys, whose fluting whistles mingled with the raucous bellow of the larger beasts and the *basso* knocking of their bells. Some were dark in colouration and many were decorated with patterned geometric markings.

The immense lake was like a picture of paradise and its view always filled me with joy and shocking incredulity, for it was as if one had slipped without any awareness out of time: so much water amidst such an extent of desert and without any human indication was exalting. It was already evapourating and its shores were growing larger and in a few months it would disappear until the next monsoon, if it came, replenished the supply. The grasses along the margin were already coppery and golden, waivering with innocent delicacy. Thousands and thousands of many species of bird were in the area or upon the water and it was as if the desert had ceased to exist as a bloodless and lifeless environment and had been strangely annulled; in its place was this immanent and unpeopled arcadia.

It is difficult to find solitude in life, not personal nor individual solitude which even in an urban setting can be acquired briefly and simply by the closing of doors or gates, but the solitude which inhabits locality itself: the perfectly transparent and ephemeral, uncaptive and untouched by human anguish or desperation, or worse, by human refuse and, even worse, by industrial waste. That was a solitude complete and unbounding which cohered about certain terrestrial circumstances, yet the apprehension of *nothing* or nil is difficult to organise or enhance, for the reduction of sensation and impulse requires a certain conceptual readiness in itself—perhaps termed as grace or initiation—or more simply, the intent when one's aim is true. For emptiness is the true state of human consciousness and ideally what one strives to become aware of as one's unity of being in the *kosmos*, even beyond light. Then, if one truly apprehends being, there is no experiencer, and only that is solitude. To experience such in the company of a friend is truly unique and sublime.

We made for a concrete platform which had been built by the Forestry Commission for the benefit of ornithologists. I had on several occasions spent afternoons and nights there and felt pleased with the familiar sight, for the structure would protect us from all the carnivores that patrolled during darkness. There were several crude tin and wooden boats beached upon the mud shore, with rudimentary oars shipped onboard. From that elevated spot for the rest of the day I studied the surrounding topography and the myriad birds with a small monocular.

Over a thousand camel were in the immediate area and I watched the herders and the women as they went about their tasks. Later, three hilarious young men arrived on an old motor-cycle and pushed one of the boats out and clumsily rowed onto the lake where they rested for a couple of hours, doubtless doing something slightly illicit and thoroughly enjoyable. To the west I could see a man up to his waist in water patrolling the shallows and casting a net. Sujaval had unpacked his light bag and taken out a tea-kit; then having prepared a hearth from three rocks and having gathered a heap of thornwood, he ignited and skillfully kindled a fire and heated the fragrant milk for tea. I was reprimanded for drinking it too speedily and not sipping it, which embarrassed me and made me once again feel churlish.

Pelican were in hundreds and far away I could discern the startling carmine gleam of flamingo, birds whose beauty I found mysterious and irresistible, for they always seemed supernatural to me. Hawks skimmed the reeds, often in pairs, back and forth for hours; painted storks waded the pools and egrets glided and paused; iridescent blue kingfishers flashed past and there were avocet and spoonbills stalking among the grasses as night herons poised motionless as they watched for small-fry. In the magenta-argent gleam of twilight thousands and thousands of cranes suddenly came streaming in low for a couple of miles in formation, filling the sky, crying and calling upon the air as they returned to the Dhand for the night. This was almost a paranormal moment, such was the extensive majesty of those minutes; its beauty was intrinsically inhuman and unearthly, as if the universe were unveiling one of its sacred views.

I had heard about what are called the *chir batti*, the 'ghost lights', and had read reports of their sightings, one of which had been written by a friend of mine, Jugal Tiwari, the distinguished ornithologist whose critical thinking I trusted. After Sujaval and I had drunken deeply of camel milk and eaten some dried millet *chapatis* which I had brought, I shawled myself against the cold and walked back onto the sands, taking a torch with me and my steely swordstick. They have been described as, "A strange light as bright as a mercury lamp that changes its color to blue and sometimes red and resembles a moving ball of fire, which sometime stops or moves as fast as an arrow. It is not just one light, but could appear at several places. The light has also been observed to become two from one. They move two or so feet above the surface of the earth."

I walked carefully for a while, uneasy in the sheer blackness of night although the heaven above was virtually a numinous and blank stellar zone. I always felt foolish carrying that swordstick even though shepherds and herders often admired its manufacture and its brass scabbard and balance; only once had I fecklessly drawn it in defence when a pariah dog had approached me one dark night when I had been walking alone. Of course the *chir batti* did not appear and if they had done I am not sure how I would have reacted, for such an irrational and unworldly experience cannot be included in this life. I would have felt a bit like young Hamlet having witnessed his father on the ramparts: what does one do with such sensations except remain silent?

I slept like iron that night, woken only infrequently by the howls and whoops of predators. Sujaval lay next to me coughing, a stone wrapped in his *ajrak* for a pillow and a light quilt covering his body. He had strewn a shallow bed of clean sand upon which to rest but he was up before the dawn, hawking and moving about for he was cold and unslept. The screams and squeal of jackal and boar—seemingly only a few feet from our heads during the black darkness—had kept him vigilant and anxious. We were both stiff and aching with the damp infiltrating cold that morning and stamped about in an attempt to warm ourselves. The Dhand was a most lucid turquoise-aquamarine tinted with a strange mineral amber and already hundreds of cranes were noisily taking to the air and circling before they set off northward once again. Day came as if dressed in tissue and its nucleus of light dilated with pleasure above the immense stretch of water. Marsh harriers were thuggishly cruising the margin of the blue lake causing much consternation among the stilts and moorhen and terns, and lapwings were beginning their inimitable cry of *did-you-do-it, did-you-do-it*. White gauze-like gatherings of a seminal dewy mist hung as phantoms or wraiths, hovering frail and flimsy. The east gently assumed a lavender hue streaked with cerise: so much overt but generously slow vitality and beneficence.

There were many fresh tracks about the platform that morning, jackal and fox and boar proliferating. I glimpsed a *nilgai* doe with a tiny grey fawn as they scampered away when I turned towards them. I saw—for what were about two seconds—a jungle cat, which I first thought was a caracal, but Sujaval shook his head, *billari*, he said. It was a large feline of golden colouration, with white and jet-black markings about its face and wispy pointed ears; that too immediately ceased to exist as soon as it observed my stare.

Dhinodhar was scarcely visible in the morning distance such was the haze of blown dust and dew. The Dhand glittered deftly and fiercely like coruscating mercury in a pre-zenith heat; it was already ninety degrees on my pocket thermometer two hours after sunrise. Our final stage of walking together was across the powdery earth, a desiccated mud of last year's monsoon when the Banni had briefly become flooded in part. The ground was crazed with miles of cracks and the deep imprints of buffalo and camel whose hooves had struggled through that wet scenery. The day was hot and windless and for once our pace felt as if it were endless and mindless as the glare was intensely dazzling; later, a mild breeze picked up the bitter saline dust and threw it about us. At Foulay the imminence of town was indicated first by a skeletal and dried cadaver of a dog lying upon the sand and then by a small open sandy area which was obviously the local boys' cricket pitch. Jagdish, my driver, was waiting at a *chai* stall, chatting with a man.

That was the end of the walk and I felt disoriented and naive, resenting the fact that my emotions and thoughts of the last two days were being forcibly diminished and eradicated as I was already forgetting all the wonderful details and instants. We greeted and drank some tea and I felt somewhat confused by the sudden overwhelming state of humanity. Sujaval became indifferent, his reserve alloyed with society; he was no longer merely a spiritual being, seemed older and less masterful. We were both unshaven and grimy with sand and stinking with odours of smoke and milk; my whole body seemed to be crammed and filmed with a minutely oily grain.

Making my farewell with Sujaval at the Nakhatrana bus station an hour or so later was terribly emotional for me. He was bound towards Bhuj and I was heading west towards Mata-No-Madh, where the tutelary deity, the goddess of all Kacch, kept her temple. We made a brief salutation of goodbye and parted. I looked back as the vehicle drove off and there was my dear companion Sujaval somewhat reticent and diffident making his way towards a ticket stand: among the rickshaw boys in their vernacular *faux*-Versace trousers and tight shirts he seemed far removed from life. He had so easily and openly shared the genius of his dignity with me and I almost wept to observe a man of such grace and extraordinary purity among such a busy and vernacular populace. This was not his loss, for he was easy, but my own, insofar as my guide and brief friend had disappeared, and such is the fragility of human affinity everywhere. His casual if not mystical decency, his art of life and its effortless independence, his natural decorum in the desert, all dissipated within that rough and hectic urban setting, filthy and messy with exhaust fumes and vile detritus.

I have accomplished many walks in my life, in different parts of the world and of varying lengths of time and my longest walk had been done in southern Greece about the peninsula of Maleas. The Banni walk had been brief and yet it had been perhaps the most exceptional and greatest of my ambulations; practically there had been nothing difficult nor complex about the recent few days, one had taken an unusual stroll, that was all. For me however, this had been one of my greatest walks, mentally and emotionally I had gone farther than ever before, and this had been mediated by association with my companion. The exquisite emptiness and unsounding world of Banni had revealed to me a beauty which I had not previously known, and that was a beauty which was very much tempered by our pedestrian manner, the two were intimately fused. Within the nature of a human soul lies that old activity of migration: that is one of our founding experiences as inhabitants of this planet and it is well that we sometimes recapitulate such movement and its creative disposition. It was on foot that we humans first encountered the pleasure and proceedings of friendship.

Yet the idea and the determination is all and achievement does not lie in the activity itself. As with swimming the Hellespont—something which I had done years before—the action required only tenacity and fitness and a certain mental flexibility or tension, a mild capacity for endurance. There is an unnameable and necessary temperament however, an urgency or longing—*pothos* is the Greek word—which impels us upon such ways: and so one goes from one to one, as it were, where it is the preconception of an activity which provides us with an unquestionable fidelity and duration.

In our conception lies the accomplishment and that point is made justly effective by speech, by words alone and not so much by behaviour; for it is through words that we cause or reach our ends, such is one of the mysteries of human culture and belief. We travel primarily in language, *via* our words, and that is the source and situation of a true journey: the practical activity is really only a *mimésis* of what exists within us as an internal vibration or weightless image, a perfectly translucent template which we bear unseen. We also travel in company and in our acquaintance with others, with person, place, and with something else that is unspeakable.

About a week later I was sitting with the Maharao of Kacch, Pragmulji III, at Ranjit Vilas, his palace in Bhuj; the building had been badly and irreparably damaged by the Two Thousand and One earthquake. We were talking about the Banni and he was telling me of times spent there during his youth earlier on in the last century, and how splendid and vast were the bird migrations in those days.

"When your son is a man," he said to me, "and that will be sooner than you think, all the world of the Banni will be gone. I give it another twenty years before the mines and industries take over and the *maldhari* flee. We shall not see it," he added sadly. "We have tried to save the panthers," he said, referring to the last few Asian leopards which inhabited his reserve at Pragsar to the west. "The government is trying to take that land now and I am not confident in what they will do there."

I recalled what another friend had once said to me, one night when we had walked out into Banni from the hamlet of Foulay and slept out on the Dhand platform. This was a young farmer called Dasharath, a scion of the Rathors, a *ksatriya* clan that was affiliated with the Maharao's Jadeja clan; his family had only come to the Kacch in Nineteen Seventy-one when conflict with Pakistan caused them to leave their lands and houses and cross the frontier. Dasharath was now a farmer with a small-holding of sixteen acres, just south of Banni.

That chilly evening as we crouched over our thornwood fire, the limitless black sky virtually nacreous with so many stars, he sang a few of his favourite *ghazals* and I had responded with a song of George Brassens and one of my own compositions, a Greek lament. We sat there in the great silence, listening to the jackals whooping behind us and to the myriad sounds of cranes and other birds that came from off the water; the darkness was tuned by the vibrant *staccato* of a million insects. A fine gibbous moon was in the air above us suspending all life in its monochrome abstract glow of zinc-coloured silvery light. Dasharath had been speaking of his dream of a moral world, where borders were no longer guarded by commandos, a world that was predictive and generous, without cruelty and friction and good for all days.

"This much has remained," he said wistfully. "For solitude has no place, there is no light to solitude; true solitude is without person, alone without name or body. So versatile and sensitive it cannot discern one thing, solitude does not forget for it has no memory. It merely presents a world, always remaining silent; beneath love's embroidered cloth it is the gentleness that breaks suffering …"

The modern genius of British travellers, a famed translator of the Homeric *Odyssey*, once wrote that, "The abstraction of the landscape cleansed me, and rendered my mind vacant with its superfluous greatness, a greatness achieved not by the addition of thought to its emptiness, but by its subtraction."

~ On Friendship ~

III ~ III

WALKING on the soft pink earth mile after mile with my wife as the great sun arched above and threw our shadows about us on the ground, we paused now and then in the shade of a banyan to drink some water, with only a few birds in the air and no other sign of life. That was my sole joy, being lone in the world with this woman and being with her in the Kacch. Only two places on earth have captured me in this way: one was Kacch and the other was in south-eastern Greece, in Lakonia, the province of Sparta.

This passion for place is something that I cannot explain, for no other environment possessed the power of exciting and thrilling me in that way. Certainly, the overtly visual was involved, for something about the perceptible form of topography in these two locations affected me profoundly, unconditionally if not morally; but it was more than the visual, another force was at work. It was not simply an optical response to linear shape for the formation of the two landscapes was different. The earth, the dust and the stones and the avid light of Kacch entered far into my being and caused a happiness unlike any other. This continues to possess me even now as I write and introduces a necessary sense of belonging to my daily consciousness; yet it is as if my wife herself were the actual medium and real location of such fervour and the tissue of language between psyche and terrain. What I am portraying here is that uniquely spousal amity which is more than and prior to the biological, or how it is that we become so uncommonly disposed in this world, as if elect.

For us, walking together had always been a paradigm of companionship, an activity where we recreated ourselves as conjoint souls in pursuit of the non-ephemeral. That peripatetic behavior where one crosses an open landscape on foot, that uncivil mobile state, was how *homo sapiens* had dwelt upon the earth long before agriculture appeared and before all neolithic settlement. It was an external condition deeply engrained in the human psyche and prior to other experience—like fire before its domestication—that preceded any fixed or sedentary life. I am not sure how far the atavistic re-occurs within human consciousness but walking for me has always remained a means to retrieve that fundamental identity, *vis-à-vis* the natural world, a consciousness that is most true. One of the initial acts in both the Hindu and the Greek Orthodox marriage rite takes place towards the conclusion of the ritual when the bride and groom take several—typically seven—paces together, hand in hand. The metaphor of walking is the proto-activity for the newly wedded pair, the original form and emblem of their joint life where the shadows of psyche might reveal themselves.

Like the celebrated twig that was taken down into the depths of a mine and left overnight in a cavern, which, on being retrieved the next day was discovered to be heavy with mineral encrustation upon its limbs, crystalline and substantial, so too does amity find adherence in the passage of time shared, the sequence of days and nights physically bound and coherent, where a man and woman offer up and exchange an unspoken momentary vision. I remember that when I first met my wife long ago in Cambridge and we began to make love together, she would never stay and sleep through the night with me, not initially.

"Sleeping with someone is far more intimate than making love," she used say. "It is a complete surrender, to be with a someone like that when one is unconscious for so many hours."

In sleep and in walking those mysterious deposits occur as we admit another unutterable world into the silent recesses of our life, where the crystals and jewels adhere and receive their physical mass. The durable gifts of the earth are only offered during such instants.

Conversely, what binds a people together as a community, as an *ethnos*, is language, not just in terms of vocabulary but also in terms of metaphor. The crises occur when signification shifts—for whatever larger reason—and then the dissimilarities in words become conflictual; people fight about meaning and kill to secure those statements. Violence becomes the order of the day within a community, as in Ahmedabad or Mumbai; for every word has its dirt just as light causes shade, and the accumulation of dirt—what a term excludes but implies—leads us into contest and dispute. Boundaries as pure abstraction emerge or dissolve and it is upon these walls that we struggle and clash. The mystery or obscurity is how words become obdurate and less fungible, what informs such sclerosis and what is the nature of the larger or containing body that effects such change? This modification which occurs in language—in terms of inclusion and exclusion, a response to some more enclosing or immuring pattern or media—supplies palpable time to history, for I think of history as just one of the many metaphors of time. There are the aeons and cycles, the *yugas*, solar and lunar time, and agricultural or migrant time which concern climate and rainfall: people receive their apprehension of time differently as the temporal manifold is always various and never simplex.

Just as implicit in a fluid compound are the planes of crystallisation and solid form, so too for language forms exist as the possible metaphors surrounding a word both in potential and yet derived from physical and material locality. Exterior causes can effect an alteration in this charge, and it is upon these margins—these are the walls—that opposition takes place. The art of liberty is one that essays to alleviate such resistance in order to maintain a maximum porosity of terms: humanism in other words. Tragedy occurs when we are no longer inclined to interpret and insist upon a single meaning.

Some would say that strife, *eris*, is a condition, if not a necessary condition of human life, and that the function of the state is to compete on a level of minimum violence to effect junctions there: junctions between the meaning of words. Only the invariance of amity, the blood-stream of friendship and mutual witness, can make things commensurate, the plea for kind and that humanistic ideal of reasonable curiosity germane to what we are not. In other words, if we are to survive we must abjure the certitude that truth is exclusive; speech and language are only devices, creative devices, and rarely function as statements of matter.

It is our facility for memory which permits us to enter into a friendship and then an affair and to be adoring, to sustain that durable light with which we have been instilled. If we are unable to recall affection received then we are unable to engage in courtship: there is only this simple transmission or equation, for the experience of emotion is in itself an unconscious recollection of past events that are being re-activated as inconscient memory. Obversely and sadly, it is the recollection of violence sustained that similarly fuels our capacity to commit a brutal act, when we deliver our suffering to others. If we can forget the horrible deeds performed during Partition—in Kashmir and the Punjab—or when the Nazis retreated from parts of occupied Europe, or what happens today in a particular Syrian camp, then the impulsion to punish cannot exist unless conditions are so appalling that one must voraciously struggle merely in order to remain. Yet how is it that we should forget, how does one destroy or rescind that vile metonymy?

Does this mean that we must not speak of horrors witnessed or experienced and permit silence to heal such wounds if it is only silence that can fully embalm our lesions and injuries? This is a silence that gangs and fraudulent politicians seek to split apart, seeking to exacerbate the cleavage and to create a wordless void that is occupied only by fearful aggression. Good friendship—being established upon an act of recognition—will always respect that kind of silence, the fathomless cavities of grief; such is the amity which occurs between warriors.

Spontaneous and uncreated love is rare if not impossible: that is, an ardour that is not informed by antecedence and the causative impetus of preceding time and which simply coheres under appropriate conditions heedless of historical weight. For human love only fulfills historical process, is part of an unfolding career that exists prior to our own lives and it possesses a potential to continue long after we are deceased, if we have loved. We are caught, and perhaps it is only the uncommon chance, if such a thing exists, for the weightless and insubstantial tissue of love is nothing but time; and obversely, the cycles and spheres of time are informed and constellated by elliptical acts of friendship.

In love we transfer our narrative or story towards another narrative that is structurally similar or ideally equal, that is all; whereas in friendship this conveyance is not so impelling but only admissible, and that provides us with a likely moment's freedom. For love, the force of narrative is paradoxically such that it is always and only bound to seek its own closure out of time, and we are caged by the necessary abstraction of those invisible words.

In India, because of the lesser importance given to material objects, particularly in traditional and non-affluent regions as the Kacch, emotional life is totally unlike emotional life in the West. In the latter society identity is always founded upon—if not attached to—material conditions: consumption and advertising play crucial roles in the construction of a persona and the self is essentially based upon an adherence and inherence of *things*. In India, due to the lack of *matériel* and the scarcity of goods the aetiology of an individual's emotional stature derives more from kinship relations than from physical relations.

Thus there is less individualism insofar as the nuclear unit is not as singular and there is simultaneously more affection and human warmth at play in social exchange. The traditional household is composed not simply by a married couple and their children but incorporates the various uncles and aunts and grand-parents and cousins who are attached to that marital unit; there is no concept of a solitary and individual who pleases his or her self and whose anomic identity is constituted generally by the purchase and display of goods and who lives with little plural responsibility. Identity here is composed of kinship affinities and emotional connections rather than *via* an appropriation of object-things that reinforce a sense of personal classification. Thus ideas of value in their generation, transmission, and reception are unlike the social values produced in the West. From this point of view the presence of such valorised if not commodified recreational sex in the West today can be viewed as simply remedial, insofar as the absence or diminution of affective life due to the disappearance of the intimately familial is conducive to such sport and its sub-culture of cinema, popular or racy vernacular literature, and nowadays immediate online and unreserved sexuality.

Looked at from another point of view, as there is little shopping to be done in the Kacch—although a small and fashionable supermarket has appeared in Bhuj recently—there is not the relationship with the *object* upon which Western individualism is founded. As the market in Kacch lacks what are known as consumer goods, objects which in Western advertising formulate what composes an individual's self-conception do not exist. Certainly, with the arrival of the cell-phone and the small motorcycle and especially with the advent of the household television set, this system or structure is beginning to change in form; virtually no village is presently without a television. Without such a vast multitude of consumer objects society there remains far more co-operative in its foundation and practice and the drive of competition is not so forceful and intractable.

Yet human personality, and not just rurally but also in the emergent towns and *bourgeoisie*, remains principally and firmly based upon kinship relations: an individual is defined by his or her grouping and not by objects. This is thoroughly unlike Western idioms of identity that are firmly grounded on the acquisition and possession of things, where personal conception and hierarchy are composed materially rather than socially or historically. Plus, traditional Kacchi society was typically non-competitive and non-acquisitive, being founded upon an hierarchic constitution; it was also a social order where marriages were not simply arranged but almost destined. In non-metropolitan areas due to the disposition towards kinship rather than to individual livelihood there is of course virtually no casual sexuality, unlike in the West where sexuality has at times become like *shopping* and is a means of repersonifying a thin and bare psychic and emotional identity. Such modes of gratification produce nothing of value in that economy of metaphors and it is as if so many empty shells merely take on a transitory but intransitive colour for a cursory amount of time, a tonal distinction that is fully evanescent.

Thus the complexity of Kacchi society is not simply due to its many ancient historical currents and the diverse order of its constitution—the various clan, caste, and religious groups—but also due to its sophisticated kinship structures. Marriages of course are always prescribed and out in the villages this can require many years of time: between the moment of initial betrothal—which sometimes occurs in childhood—and before an exchange of dowry is fully complete and the bride finally crosses her new threshold. Some communities still practice child marriage, but discreetly, as this is legally improper nowadays. There are few rare exceptions among the rising and educated or professional middle class where couples do marry for love, but this is not promoted and inter-caste marriage is unusual as it means matrimony beyond one's natal or religious terrain.

The only civic unrest that occurred in Mandvi in the Twentieth century was occasioned by a crisis caused by the discovery of a Moslem youth courting a young Hindu girl; for the latter group this was wholly unacceptable and in fact dangerous. In Kacch, adulthood for a man begins with marriage, but for a woman this transition is marked by the birth of a child, particularly a son; there is this strong asymmetry between the male and feminine.

It is thus the kin-group which dominates communal life, unlike what obtains in much of the West where the idea of the freely mobile individual is paramount. In contemporary Kacch the social unit is the extended family and not the singular being for a person only flourishes within a conjugal group and nowadays this extends to cousins in East Africa or the Gulf or to fraternal kin in North America, to all the members of a band as well as to those further social unions from whom brides and grooms are received. Often in other parts of the South Asia these kinship formations of caste succeed well in burgeoning industrial economies where they perform as fraternal capital supplying dynamic infrastructure to new capitalist ventures, a phenomenon which has transferred to migrants in Britain and North America.

There is more love, in other words, in India, and love that is unrestricted; nor does the phantasy of required romantic love preclude keen emotions of attachment. Marriages can be and are arranged because the sustenance of love is not laid upon a phantasm of illusory individuality, itself founded upon a near-autonomous series of object-relations. Love in the Sub-Continent—or much of it—is a different story therefore, compared to what is heard and seen in the West. The two forms of narrative are entirely dissimilar and un-like in how they combine living bodies, for apart from such romance the human frame does not actually exist: anatomy without language has no destiny whatsoever, even pictorial language.

Thus the emotional life of the Kacch differs markedly from what obtains in the West; this is also the case for much of modern India although the Kacch being far more conservative and orthodox and having only a small and non-consuming middle class manifests this paradigm more succinctly and inflexibly. This is changing however, with great rapidity. Not so long ago the bicycle was seen as a middle-class vehicle, then the lightweight motor-cycle began to dominate the roads; now it is the small automobile which is the cynosure of rising status and acquisitiveness.

In a prior chapter about migration and walking I attempted to portray human affection and its pursuits and there I focussed on one particular model of the feminine as being key to the entire formulation of Western amity, that of the *femme fatale*. Such a psyche perhaps exhibits the purest form of consciousness—almost animal-like in its original integrity and pre-morality—without the accretions of complex language; even awareness is virtually occluded except for a permanent and oblique condition of doubt.

I suppose that historically this is due to such individuals—both men and women—being severely inhibited at some point early on in their cerebral and verbal development when the natural evolution of emotion became barred and so the usual vehicles of cognition became precluded. Needless to say it is my firm presumption that the feminine takes all priority in the formation of any human amity, and here, the idea of the *femme fatale* was the primary metaphor. Naturally, this is an image which could actually be applied to both men and women, to the male and to the feminine, for by these terms I do not only mean *woman*, I mean a kind or manner of agency and not an active biological personality.

For me, the model of the *femme fatale* is a picture of emptiness and of living void and is atavistic. As we observed elsewhere it is the zero or nought which can be perpetually moved among any series of ciphers in order to change the quantities concerned. If metonymy is the nature of how such a psyche functions there is little access to metaphor in that state, for such a life is only and necessarily serial, constantly attaching itself to things or other persons who are themselves the subject of things. For those kinds of people, and not only women in particular, sexuality and the sensual charge given to the human body are greatly controlling: therein lies the wealth of a corporeal economy whence value is created, *via* the creation and privileging of pleasure and genital sensation.

As with Don Juan, the emotional market of such a person is one that desperately and repetitiously seeks to find a single value in a life, for he or she is destitute of all received valence. One could describe Don Juan as a *femme fatale*, someone who is frantically seeking for just one dependable and substantial sign: he is a pure and unresting phenomenologist, an hypothetically presocial man.

Love in India is different, there is no *femme fatale* in that culture—although by India I suppose that I actually mean the Kacch and perhaps Saurasthra—and the absence of such a void is substituted by the extraordinary complex patterning which large and extended kinship structures provide. Human life is extremely different in that part of the globe in comparison to the West and my wife remarked on several occasions how there was never anything at stake for

Kacchi men; there was no performative necessity by which their masculinity was driven as there is in Greece or France. Kacchi masculinity nowadays evinces far greater emotional range than anything that is to be observed in the West. The same can be said of Kacchi womanhood.

In some of these pages I have tried to trace how—given the nature of the *femme fatale* and the vacance of such an individual—if weight is not available to objects and to things and to consumption, then landscape and its topography become active in the organisation of identity; such is the germ of tourism. Passion for place is perhaps the only truthful fortune for the alienated Westerner unless they convert—and that process is mysterious—their disaffection and estrangement and retrieve what is their inheritance: the unique and rare contact with another human being upon which all life and optimism is founded. This becomes an ideal type for humanism and friendship and is what is popularly referred to in the liberal press today as 'deep-ecology'. William Wordsworth in his self-revelatory poem the *Prelude* portrayed how his district environment was vitally instrumental in his own childhood and education.

In other words, for those who have lost their original kinship formation through migration, schismatic modernism, urbanism, or through subjective loss—the affinity and affiliation of family, the tissue that envelops the personal and which creates a persona—there exists the possibility that place, terrain or situation, can supply the prime metaphors leading to desire and expression. These, by filtering language and speech, enable an individual to become aware of his or her self, so granting a concomitant sense of efficacy in time and the world.

For the individual is a fine illusion, a false mirror or membrane which only projects a quality or aspect of *trompe l'oeil* upon the lexical screen of a human psyche: that is something in its abstraction which is akin to the infinitely proliferating idea of a market economy which is so implicit and paradigmatic for the modern West. We can move beyond our inherited and incorporated selves but this is mysteriously uncommon and not actually elective.

Cattle feed upon grass, sheep and goat browse and forage for shrub and vegetation, camel graze upon thornier and more desert-like but palatable plants: so an environment imposes conditions upon those who rear such animals and it is not simply landscape itself which generates metaphor within a language but also the means of production by which a people thrive or survive therein. The system of living itself is causative of metaphor, myth, and of language, and one can even posit that geology ultimately affects literature and that a respected landscape possesses a humanising quality in itself. Within such a firm material or mineral context the behaviour and manners of friendship—and not of love—are what truly elicit our deepest and greatest humanity, and our presence in a certain terrain is part of this enhancement and potential magnitude.

There is a hill, a small mountain, south of the Banni area of Kacch and the Chari Dhand marsh, called Nanamo. It is a former volcano about which much cultivation and herding takes place and for those who dwell in the region it is a focal part of their panorama. For distant mariners at sea however, Nanamo stands out like a great beacon—what MacMurdo, an early traveller to the region and the first British Resident, described as a giant sugar-loaf—powerful in its definition and remarkable distinction, providing them with an indubitable bearing.

For me, human amity has always been of a similar mettle. When one is close and within its vicinity it is not obvious and its being not always conspicuous. From afar however, when one is alone upon a wonderful sea or ocean, friendship—upon which love can at times be amplified—appears as the organising principle of all one's mental field: palpable, thoroughly evident, and the principal landmark to all transitions.

~ On Friendship ~

IV ~ I

WALKING on ice is unlike walking in any other environment, unlike walking in the desert or through hills or across a plain. Visually, audially, and in terms of security it is a completely different experience, and in these parts of the world generally briefer due to the fierce cold and to the physical smallness of the frozen New England lakes.

For us recently, this has been a winter where—at week-ends—we have driven westwards out of town and visited the various ponds in which we had often swum during warmer seasons. It was only in the early new year when the mercury in the thermometer sank well below zero *fahrenheit* that we were able to venture out across those solidified waters, something we had never encountered before. Those were the theophanic days of the Magi, silent and withdrawn into a great natural sleep with all the landscape at rest and internal to itself. One could almost hear in that dense impeccable quietness the ring of bridle chains and stamp of hooves as those mythical travellers approached across printless fields of snow and rocks of ice.

Early one Sunday morning in late December my wife and I had gone out to Walden in order to amble in the woods. We had frequently circumambulated the pond during the autumn months but on this occasion conditions were changed, for when we crossed the road and were looking down upon the water we found another lake. Instead of the usual subtlety of lucid celadon and viridian the surface of the pool flashed and crackled with reflected terse and impermeable light; white blazes and sparks appeared to be shooting up from the water, serene and tranquil.

We tentatively walked out onto the dense shell of the solidified lake, sliding and slipping as the plateau of ice twanged and reverberated with a deep uncanny sound beneath our feet as long grey tendril-like fractures embedded within the translucence bent and shifted. The ice was still growing and straining so the sounds of its groans and thrumming were constant and also alarming. Two indistinguishable skaters were dashing back and forth, dribbling and passing a puck, far away towards the centre of the lake; a solitary ice-fisherman was visible in the distance as a dim speck, cutting a hole into the water with a large screw.

We skirted the pond and slowly returned, amazed by the sensation of being somewhere normally forbidden; one's view of the terrain about was completely altered. Now and then the skaters sped past, their blades hissing with a noise that was like tissue being torn and the youthful pleasure which they exhibited in their skill of movement was beautiful to watch, balletic and agile. The sharp turquoise light was so strong and bright that they appeared as black speeding creatures, abstractly synchronised.

This was the only time that we ever witnessed a frozen lake where the ice was still green, glassily transparent and exposed. On that morning we had caught the perfect instant—just after the freezing of the water and before snow or frost caused the icy plane to become blanched and coarse. One could peer down into the depths and near the margins gaze at the bottom where stones and logs and sometimes slow-moving shady trout were visible in a turgid gloom. The ice must have been at least a foot thick, a glazed translucent green, like beryl or watery emerald.

At White Pond, our second walk upon the ice, the situation was completely different. A friend of mine—someone with whom I row upon the Charles in summer—had told us of this spot, recommending it for privacy and isolation and for the purity of its swimming during hot weather. Never having visited the place before we had to first drive for an hour about the area, poring over a map, trying to locate the site for it was sunk in a *petite* hollowed valley.

On that day we observed a couple of hawks languidly crossing the cobalt air; usually there were never any birds about as the temperature was so terrifically low and inimical to life. There were also a couple of ice-fishermen standing motionless beside their holes and as they wore an enormous quantity of clothing they appeared as large, shapeless, and mildly sinister figures. Never did they seem to change their setting and they were always alone and individual. The lake was otherwise completely deserted, all was space and brittle metaphysical light, the phenomenal brilliance of the sun charged and reflected upward by the icy mirror into a sheer and empty cerulean sky. We had to keep walking in order to stay warm.

We returned to White Pond the next week when the temperature had risen slightly. Then, we able to stay longer as the cold was not so oppressive. Unlike Walden, there were a few houses on the edges of the water—although deserted and locked at that time of the year—and after walking we took two deck-chairs from one terrace and went out upon the ice to sit. For a while we watched a couple of skaters and the few motionless fishermen. The sense of pure volume without perspective was satisfying to the eye, along with the clarity of the air and its pristine sterility as the sheets of ice below us groaned softly like deep wires being strummed. Around us along the periphery of the lake the blackness of the forest was as if a dense two-dimensional surface. There was no consciousness apparent among the motionless bare trees or in the birdless static air, only an unearthly and paramount radiance of icy whiteness. The beauty of so much perfect immobility was almost unbearable such was its palpable transience, for no matter how long one watched and observed the scene its inhuman serenity was always elusive and evaded any mere act of human cognition. The soft milky blueness of the heaven entered one and cancelled all thoughtfulness or emotion, inhabiting us both extensively and completely. Profoundly empathetic and yet without inward contention or reciprocity, absolutely lacking in volition, and yet in no way passive or without altruism, that view which we walked about—crossing and recrossing the sheeted skin of frozen water—was nevertheless mysteriously alert and reflective with an inexpressible candid and charismatic lightness.

At Flints Pond, the third occasion for our walking upon ice, the extent of the lake was different, being a much larger and more open body of water. It was a long walk with a variety of foresting: meadow with willow, fringes of birch, pine wood, and copses of ash. There, no sign of human life existed and there were no birds. Sometimes tracks went out across the lake—which was over a mile in breadth and length—of fox or some other small quadruped. For a while we remained within the trees, keeping to a path. At one point we came upon a large brown boulder with a bronze plaque set into it. Inscribed were a few lines commemorating the death of a young woman who had disappeared into the ice a decade previously, one January; her body had never been retrieved. Perhaps there were springs beneath the lake which weakened the surface in parts and she must have walked upon one of those fragile areas. As a result, we never reached far out onto that lake despite the tantalising beauty of the situation with its rare splendour of void and absolute whiteness. It was as if we were circumscribing on foot an idyllic and unapproachable land: nothing was visible there and yet its beauty was totally implicit. We stared upon that colourless vacancy, possessed by its complete lack of sign and concomitant superlative luminosity.

It was entirely desolate of any movement except for swirls of snow-dust that gently traversed the skin of the water; sometimes they spun in slow rising vortices as they moved across the steep and tenuous light. At another point, we halted and watched a great dark stain shifting almost imperceptibly, as if something was carefully and tediously moving beneath the ice, a current or some vast bubble easily at home beneath that absolutely proscribed and hazardous place.

Some days later, during the week, we went out towards Concord and drove toward the marshes of Great Meadows. There, all was silence and unbounded radiance, birdless and without token of human life. The sky was unruffled and still without the usual sound of jets passing overhead and the atmosphere was a gleaming blue as the ice of the shallow lake reflected that tone back to us. All about we were circled by a ring of dun sandy-coloured fields of reed, vibrating and rattling in the breeze. It was as if we were walking upon an invisible depthless surface of azure, enclosed by an annular band of dry grass: all was firmament and chaste light, weightless, as we walked and floated in the glare, enclosed by a narrow belt of land. Later, to the north, geese occasionally rose up noisily from the Concord river and wheeled above those woods, obviously disturbed by something.

Now and then the ice faintly cracked with a dull splintering resonance and in places there were thin pools of grey water. In other parts were the hidden remains of muskrat nests, raised heaps of mud and twig. That day we did not go far out onto the marsh, but stayed close to the stale reed-beds. The experience was one of extraordinary numinosity and brilliance, intensified by the cold. It took us several hours afterwards—and numerous cups of tea in a café—to warm up our bodies. Of all our walks upon ice, this one had been the most overwhelmingly beautiful and sublime, and returning to the urban terrain of Cambridge was somewhat unpleasant and dis-spiriting; for we were surrendering the complete spaciousness of Great Meadows, that sense of immaterial refinement, of being momentarily immanent and without quality, and resuming a diurnal and imperative consciousness.

Punkatassett was the site of our last ice walk, for spring was creeping towards Massachusetts and it was February; the inclination of the light was further north and the air had warmed and was more damp, less desiccated by the cold. This was the smallest of all the lakes and a *milieu* that beaver favoured; it was also where the finest and most aged foresting could be found, immensely tall and slender pines that swayed in the strong north-easterlies, swishing and murmuring through the air. The trunks of those trees were old and large, like ships' masts, strong and firm, unlike the secondary-growth of young pines about Walden or White Pond.

As we approached the lake we passed over a fissure in the earth where the frozen snow had split open and revealed a rapidly flowing stream; it was like peering into a tiny crack in a glacier. At the brim of the lake there were small pools and runnels of liquid water and we did not walk out onto the ice at all until towards the end of our walk when we saw an ice-fisherman. Presuming that such persons were expert in judging ice density we wandered in his direction; as we did so another couple appeared at the other end of the pond with some dogs who noisily raced around, barking and skidding.

This time there was no sound issuing from the stiff surface, no crackling nor ringing. The air no longer possessed that moistureless quality of cavernous winter and there was a sweet vernal feeling to the place, a hint of the possibility of warmth. From the woods came the occasional song of birds, small birds, and there were many tracks upon the frost, principally of deer. We knew that we would not be doing this again, that in the coming days and weeks the ice would melt and become precarious and dangerous. Having initially detested the awful coldness of recent weather we now felt a sadness at the imminent conclusion to our strange and exclusive winter rambling; this had been so unbearably frigid at times and yet so expansive and uninhibited, senseless with an acute severity, leaving us with our own small and impressionable duality. The walks had transported our thoughts and feelings elsewhere to a place where language and image did not exist and it was as if we had together touched upon the origins of psyche and the first moments or steps of human awareness.

This winter, the river Charles—like the lakes, even though it was a moving water—had frozen hard and dark. As a rower, during the course of many years I knew every detail of that river except for this new and rigid state; yet being part of a municipal setting, to walk out upon the water was prohibited and the police enforced that ruling. We have friends—older people—who spoke of chills long ago in Cambridge when it had been possible to skate all the way up to Watertown and back upon the river, a distance of eight miles, but this was no longer permitted; I had witnessed young couples on skis being given tickets for their transgression. Swimming—diving off the Weeks Bridge—was now similarly banned during the summer.

Down where the stream opened out into a basin, beneath the skyscrapers of Boston, a great flat topography of frozen water developed in the new year. In previous cold seasons I had sometimes walked along the inland shore-path, always in the early mornings when the sun was low and rising from behind the glass towers of the city, shooting out long citron rays like giant and titanic beams. Then, the ice had run through the whole range of the chromatic spectrum, from pink to green, to blue and indigo. I had always wanted to walk across the river but of course it too was illicit.

This year, not long after the solstice, some of the students at MIT—probably from the arts department—had gone about the town and collected all the abandoned and disjected Christmas trees. One evening when the police were off-watch, they had taken these and, going out onto the water had bored holes for the stems and planted the trees in the ice so that there appeared to be a coppice of pine saplings.

How lovely it was to see that sudden copse out there on the barren face of the frozen waste: a uniquely green area of foliage. The undergraduates had made their plantation near to one of the bridges and one Sunday we walked out and looked down upon the novel grove. The artificiality of the sight was exquisite, there was something so charmingly unreal and impossible to the view, in profoundly harmonious counterpoint to an hostile extreme. A few birds were about, having found shelter in the trees.

For us, walking upon the ice of those congealed and whitened lakes encapsulated the utter depth and compression of winter, with its visual remoteness and elimination of sensation and its powerful infertile coldness. Perception became minimal in such an environment, reduced to a narrow superficial area between the stark sapphire blueness of pure sky and the arid white horizontal of gelid water; all this being fringed with a dark green periphery of evergreen and birch and ash.

Due to the lack of stimuli in such locations and the vigour of the cold, walking on ice is a contemplative activity. There is little to attract one's attention and—as in meditation or prayer—the mind is ideally suspended without consciousness. So it was during those brief walks as we patrolled the growling and chafing surface only a foot above an inhospitable depth below, always with the possibility that the ice might fissure and crack and we would be gone. During those short promenades one's mental and emotional state similarly assumed a form of suspense. We made those walks not as individuals but as two companions for whom those joined paces were steps that remained at the heart not simply of a friendship but of a certain espousal, for this was the origin of a new awareness for us both, of amity within a pure unoccluded cell of natural life.

Being asked about their happiness, some people recall commensality and how it is when they dine with dear friends, others recollect their love-making, their old houses, or their most beloved animals, but for us those hours passed on foot together lay at the heart of our complete company. Those efforts to perceive the sublime within a landscape which now and then we made were intrinsic to all the rest of life and were akin to milestones along a perpetual way: personal, terrestrial, and if successful—which was not always the case—touching upon an absolute condition.

We were like those fishermen who, hooded, cowled, and faceless in the intense bright day, stood poised and covert upon the membrane of ice as it played and flexed musically, cracking and twanging with the motion of water sealed beneath its single plate. Those men and women—as they silently imagined the life, habits, and inspissate ways of the fish beneath them, calculating and seducing with their nylon lines and hooks—those figures, in their reserved concentration, focussing upon the darkness beneath their feet, resembled us in how we live and shift so casually and unconsciously throughout time, projecting ourselves into the future.

For we too attempt to discern the nature of what we do not know and above which we are so delicately and mentally suspended, separated by a mere pane of solid pellucid matter which at any instant might break and precipitate us into an endlessly thoughtless and impenetrable blackness where human consciousness has not ever occurred.

~ On Friendship ~

IV ~ II

HOW is it that if all our knowledge is derived and our understanding is always and only to be received from another life or person, especially from those to whom we are psychically and emotionally close, how is it then that we certainly live, that is, if we are fully recipient of all consciousness and are without an originally effectual state? This is a most potentially damning statement governing what it means to be human, for how on earth can we escape such a view of time and not merely arise, flourish, and then perish as if we were simply conduits and conductors lacking a capacity for autonomous reflection or deviation? This is not merely a question concerning the possibility of innovation or invention nor is it a case that stands against any notion of possible volition but is a comment on the nature of experience, both social and physical, and a meditation upon human achievement. There will always be a seed and there are always tracks but these are not always overt or possessing distinction; yet nothing exists without antecedence and certainly, not any idea.

The movement of plants and of animals is initially evolutionary and then becomes recipient in a structural and mediate sense, whereas the changes within the contemporary human psyche and its actions are caused through more historical or prior settings. Almost all of human activity is reiterative and neither creatively sovereign nor motive and these two kinds of determinative agency possess two different mental and affective states of impulsion.

The phenomenon of the *femme fatale* participates in this evolutionary standard and in its most spotless profile is necessarily *echolalic*, bound to repeat verbally, mentally, or even in terms of manner, what is most immediate; for such a figure lacks all preference or decision. Narcissism is a regular mode for these men and women as their fashion of being is innately remedial and defensive, drawing on the objective world as a means of psychic provision or fuel and so fulfilling their personal void. The *femme fatale* is terrifically friendless and desperately in search of amity and, as such presents a type of archaic psyche, one that is usually confined by genital contact.

How does one become an independent friend with another human being and, what occurs between those two engaging persons; what is the medium of that affinity which is neither natural nor physiological—unlike human love and affection—but elective and selective. According to our express definitions the bearing of friendship is most discerning and the most necessarily discriminating and percipient instant of all wakeful and alert cognition. I would argue that it is this particular affective connectivity or living mental tissue which supplies us with a perfectly discrete knowledge of life and its means of recollection.

Yet if we are only what we have received how is this act of freedom—the act of friendship—actually possible? It is a paradox and somehow we need to go beyond ourselves to resolve the dilemma. To repeat: evolution, recipience, and election are the three trajectories that cause human sentience, yet it is the last of this triad which is most enigmatic and inscrutable for it is without palpable purpose. We might plainly rephrase this historical series as nature, culture, and apperception.

Now in conclusion let us examine seven summary moments of force that encompass such an hypothetical model, centripetally drawing together what we have delineated in the preceding pages.

Firstly, if the perception of an admired landscape or a mutual exchange of humane and moral affection are the two axiomatic and primary leagues of experience which we possess, allowing us to generate or employ images, does one actually receive these conditions as either unique or unqualified; or, are we ourselves only vehicles—metaphors—of what has long been established and evolved, and our source of expression is just another transitional or traditional receipt of which we are truly unaware? The vital question then would be, what is convened here that is causative of a capacity to create metaphor insofar as nothing is superfluous?

It is my assertion that is it not only the principles of human affinity—the immutable core of *philía*, 'friendship'—but also the attractive nature of a *locale* or environment which is profoundly instrumental in the organisation of metaphor for human life. The pages of this book illustrate that activity. By metaphor I do not mean simply the utility of images—one representing another, *this* for *that*—but more generally, in that all activity is metaphor and vehicular and where even sexuality itself, something which we consider to be personal and individual, is also only rhetorical.

True friendship exceeds metaphor, *via* its awareness of metaphorical operation, and this is akin to the distinction which exists between images and fine painting, for the latter will always transport the viewer towards a condition which is not actually present nor immediate. Friendship is of this latter category and concerns the status of election.

I would strongly aver that human friendship and the equally valid attraction, passion, and appreciation for natural beauty are the essential dual instruments which conduce to the establishment of humanistic consciousness in the world. These emotional and material environments revive our original impulses which refract in the human mind and capture time for an instant upon a steel glass of recollection and anticipation. These are the media which enable us to go away from our evolved selves and all that has been only received; for it is during such incidents of amity or during such instants when we apprehend the beauty of a certain panorama that we might become briefly elected and removed from a certain nature of inevitable repetition. Such constitutes our most singularly small circumstance of potential liberty.

These paradigmatic ideas of exceptional *praxis* likewise hover in time insofar as they are repeated as forms and formalities represented not only in experience but most particularly in literature, *re-minding* us of lost but cohering events that have been refined and verified by art and its creative exertion. Literature and painting bring to us these patterns, emotive experience, registry, events, and moments which we can revisit without needing to recall anything; there is no labour in such literal experience. Reading and pictorial representation at a certain point in human history became an active condition of experience itself where one could travel from continent to continent with swiftness and flair.

Secondly, once there was a preliterate era, an heroic world which was overruled by a vision of *fame* where songs maintained authority and human knowledge could approximate to those moral situations, both for inspiration and for substance. That too, as a dynamic, was also a manner of recipience, in terms of human experience and expression; for being then, in an antique and fully non-secularly conceived world was permeable and open to images and perceptions which were pre-discursive and not to be spoken or said, for in that aeon human mnemonics were not simply linguistic but also efficaciously ritual.

Similarly, the conception of human interval in those days was pre-temporal and circular, prior to the linear and individual qualities of the metonymical and prosaic; for only with the invention of writing and of prose systems came the introduction of procedures where grammar and syntax were clearly metonymical, just as with the use of *specie* or money. Writing brought with it a subsequent cognisance of serial and sequential time and therefore a different set of emotional efficiency.

There, in the quasi-utopia of a preliterate and premonetary era, time was constituted simply by the repetition of the sun's shadow and the imitations of earthly labour; the activity of imagination was limited and defined by the drama of the unit form of the year, typically an agricultural or ergonomic year. Yet we cannot return to or even intellectually retrieve those moments before neolithic settlement when the cultivation of land became established, not even hypothetically: when fire was domesticated, mineral tools first knapped, and human society and language began to cohere in repetitive reference and hierarchy. Landscape and the physical environment were then the initial ground for human expression, impelling a situation where amity was first intentionally and willfully rather than necessarily exchanged. In those early ages human consciousness was not distinct from natural causes and movement within the environment and humanity was still part of the animal kingdom. I like to think of human language then as being akin to the character and traits of birdsong, it was sonorous but not melodic.

Knowledge in those preliterate and premonetary times was grounded upon a profound admiration of place or affection for person or perhaps animals. Nevertheless, knowledge was still derived and never primarily immediate; that was the dilemma, for only the deities in such an aeon could experience any original degree of truth, for truthfulness in those days was simply a case of *not-forgetting* rather than anything inferential or deductive.

Then, the division between what was natural and what was spoken or enacted did not exist and human affection was simply a matter of repeating a possible binary variation, it was mimetic and *eidetic*, for being was so thoroughly informed. In later times, to distinguish between action and destination was perhaps the one fractured instant of consciousness that supplied us with an illusion of determinative volition and distinction; and therein lay the hypothetical origins of any solemn rite.

Thirdly, when life is no longer conceived as cyclical and the ends of life are no more given at the beginning of time, the future does not amplify the past and there is no equilibrium of difference any more. Then, what are the principles that define how kinship and friendship are aligned, what are the archetypes of that circumstance and its qualities?

Likewise, in such a *milieu*, what would be the sources of beauty and of the unspeakable energy that beauty drives? For certainly an understanding of an aesthetic in some way or another is the basis for companionship to become viable and vivacious even if this is not epiphanic: the sublime of not merely physical or material form but of intellectual, moral, or sentimental magnetism. It is this discernment of abstract harmony that truly fires and sustains friendship according to reciprocal desire. True companionship hovers upon such an equivalence which is so fundamentally generative that it goes beyond all recipience, mutually and simultaneously flowing like an invisible and weightless fluid rather than being simply fungible; for syllogistic distinction at this point possesses just one similar or *like* emotional charge or valence.

Hence our metaphors of close kinship and of beauty are raised upon an appreciation of such implicit affection and of terrain. This is our presence in material and earthly topography, a paradise of letters and of poetry or, the original place of idyll where one begins to become conscious. Obversely, there the possibility of allure and of guilt, of domination and of mendacity also arises out of perverse obscurity; ironically, guilt does own an inscrutable attraction insofar as it conduces to a separation of awareness, what is in fact an appreciation of injustice.

Yet is it possible that the creativity of life on earth is fallible, that evolution is not simply efficient and that error is feasible in time? By error I do not mean the random or fortuitous but inexplicable personal consequence. Certainly, one accepts that social liberty is founded upon a ground established by animal or climatic coercion and that freedom is thus only for the frugal. Given such potential constraints that environ us how then does the phenomenon of human alliance exist within such a field? For evolution occurs not simply within a state of limit and negation but also within a frame of identity and community and along that axis lies the relationship between mineral terrain and human fondness.

So what are the causal links here that circulate not simply about the state of amity but also around our sense of an aesthetic? Works and days concern *both* place and person and our criteria are—I would submit—initially appealing and relate to an awareness of what constitutes the beautiful: that which best composes our survival and which is effortless to thought, for the beautiful is proximate and unbrokered and requires no representation.

Without friendship we are lost or our solitude is mandated to assume cosmic proportions which then generalise affinity to levels that are absolute and inhuman; perhaps there is something profoundly appointed in that. Hence there is a curious natural selection at play in the origins of company and amity, both in time and in physical relation, and it is as if an outlandish or unusual gravity were at work, uniting and conveying, so that the social can operate in a more intimate or private state, one that abjures metaphor.

Fourthly, and to continue with this mythically pragmatic note, if human love concerns reproduction then friendship is a matter of work, a labour which creates an object of value; or, how effort brings together partnership as a metaphorical golden epoch becomes silvery and a place where worth is distinctly apart from *things*. That shift from the golden to the silver age marks a concomitant movement where human values originate and take their first pace, becoming aware of the potential which grief introduces into the world, for there is no moral death nor labour in the golden time and all of life exists in a state of perfect and endurable amity. I would suggest that our sensibility for company and for beauty precedes any ethical understanding and partakes of an evolutionary aspect, one that recalls that first mythical generation.

In the days of original *muthos* during the golden time when all human paradigms were first developing there was no need to create value and neither work nor sexuality existed for the natural world was then thoroughly beneficent and utopic. In the silver age, a time of idyll and the pastoral and also a period of transhumant or recurrent migration, human affection existed without any of the clouding and occlusion which immoveable property supplies. Affinity was then without object and fully emotional, no thing intervened in that solely pedestrian life and yet death had appeared along with its gifts of sorrow. To be aware then was only to co-operate.

Fifthly, and to return to our initial question, how is it then that human amity is possible in an original sense or field if all of life and familiarity are received and only derivative; are human beings so completely and imperatively co-ordinated by reception? In that case what is it which makes for creativity or our capacity to designate metaphor: is it that refinement is all and there exists no question of priority or is it that virtue lies in the perfection of thought rather than in any attempt at illusive invention as human beings are thoroughly recreational and without true volition? If we inhabit a complete desert how is it that life receives its first marks or display?

Perhaps our only solution or possible elevation occurs either in a state of admiration for the truly radiant or in respect of an undemanding and gratuitous love, or, in our solitary ambulations through a bare landscape. Only these two activities authentically recapitulate our real and essential psychic bearing. For if all of life is a situation of absolute recipience and inheritance then all of life is necessarily unified: this is our most fundamental and profound zero or ground.

Then the perception of a singular and cohering idea is our only culminating destiny, that is the crux, even if it were a fully aniconic monotheism. It is the perception of this moment which supplies us with our isolated brief potential for freedom or, for what we have been referring to as *friendship*, with place and with person. Both of these moments of emotive force necessarily admit of the beautiful.

The one mysterious question which remains therefore is, who are those who become aware of such union and is this condition optional? As they patrol the uninhabited natural world these ones grow to understand the inherent lack of intellectual and conceptual fission which exists in a landscape of *flora* and *fauna*. If beauty consists in the profoundly coherent then love becomes inevitable: such was the Dantean view of *kosmos*. Natural affinity and elective affinity are thus not only alike and akin but insofar as they contribute to the generation of psychic metaphor they both originate and sustain human consciousness. Elective affinity however, will always exceed any form of ritual, whereas natural affinity can be formalised.

Sixthly, without our friends we are not even tinkling cymbals and in that view even the idea of a family is not biological but amicable if it is to succeed in conveying the matrix of its truth. It is ironic that ideal knowledge is thus a retreat from thinking, a withdrawal from the social and mental life of humanity and a recoil towards the truly earthly and supernal; this is not sexual but conscient. Perfection here lies in and at the junction of companionship, the presence of a beloved companion who walks beside one in a pre-social and ethical terrain, mutually conscious of that single invisible and unitary candescence which informs us long before we accept any other idea. This is real espousal.

Without friendship and a shared sense of how beauty encloses us with both ephemera and an accompanying indication of the absolute, we cannot exist. The urbane, the secular, and the unduly individual, simply admit to a possibility for great error where friendship is strictured and beauty is neither immediately available nor productive, for there natural agency is precluded and denied. Somehow we need to make this stealthy and enigmatic election if we are to claim any touch of humanity and that remarkable association where duality or doubleness becomes our most earthly situation, where causative nature becomes the foundation of our inward culture or psyche.

Here, friendship is not amorous love for—as we have argued—that kind of ardent relation is founded upon an imperative sequence whereas true attraction among human beings is established by the effort and conception of what it means to be human: we become aware of what we are not. Friendship and *amor* do of course at times converge and cohere but they are originally distinct forms of awareness; amorous life can only be thoroughly repetitive whereas amity is progressive. By election though, I do not mean an active and purposeful movement but rather, the more strangely passive and experienced understanding of election itself, of being that is covertly elected; this is inexplicable and surreptitious.

It is that small catch of beauty—a hook or binding—which draws our attention away from its capsule of timeless habitation, the beauty of a friend or the beauty of a landscape which causes psyche to move away from its interminably iterative self. By *beauty* I do not mean the tangibly physical or embodied but rather the intrinsic and inherent perception of a moral aesthetic which is integral to that kind of amicable or pedestrian attraction. This is something which is unseen and unobserved for those who are not privy to such a kind of mental and affective action of the conceptually tactile. In this light our ephemeral apprehension of beauty will always possess the force of goodness, when we see with our eyes closed.

Lastly, and ancillary to the above, heroes in epic literature are often typically portrayed as creatures of great physically integral beauty and as possessing an inexhaustible capacity for varying patterns of awareness; the personal amity that obtains among heroes is often more significant—emotionally—than that which is directed at the spouse, ancestor, or offspring which simply repeats models and paradigms. This degree of potential amity is especially true between heroes and their charioteers.

Our earlier model of the *femme fatale* who, desperate for a single metonym to grasp onto in a world where metaphor is denied, lies at the heart of this evolutionary process and one can view such an hypothetical instant as an heroic age, an epoch that once lay upon the broad and beveled cusp between golden and silver generations of myth. Conceptually, Odysseus would precede Achilles for the mariner struggles not to be alone, whereas heroic Achilles embraces cosmic solitude as being the only possible sign of undying and indestructible life.

For the modern hero, giving is more important in life than receiving—not in a material nor emotional sense but ideally so—and they are the true heroes who are able to offer and to implement more than they accept or collect from life. That is the only truly ultimate freedom of which we might become conscious, that cordial and interior sphere of perception which is hypostatic to an act of unforgettable friendship: an estate which is generative rather than acquisitive.

For such an action of affective intimacy is our most profound and ineradicable condition in this world and our only honest state of personal liberty. Friendship is both optional and decisive and is also not necessary, we receive its benison in the same fashion that we admit to the overwhelming perfection of the natural world and both of these events create an initial sensibility for moral obligation in a succession of days. Conversely, if we are lacking such commitment or responsibility for another we cannot truly declare ourselves to be human. For human amity, most certainly, can travel a thousand miles in a few seconds, just like a hawk.

As a rider to all the above, in this light one can think of Byron or Gauguin or even of the cinema of Wenders, artists who created—through fiction or visual illusion—a world that is more true than ordinary and diurnal experience. They went further than mere topography or human *ethos* towards the refinement of an ideal community and landscape which—being beautiful—was thus more than true and more proximate to the nature of the durable. Such artists depicted or represented a society in which human experience was played out as design in order that something of the anonymous, enigmatic, and the concomitant emptiness of human life might be better delineated: a little more conspicuously or delicately, made more familiar and so simultaneously tireless.

For if human values are only arrangements and systems of received signs that is all that any art form might ever attempt to perfect, creating a beautiful lens through which one might perceive a possibly truer world: for art is not life. That for me is the true mastery of any excursion, when one approaches the margins and borders of human experience and observes a severely fresh or untold sight, acquiring novel proficiency there. It is only light, shadow, and perspective which causes beauty to exist.

Like the Socratic fish that put its head out of the water and saw 'the true sky, the true light, and the true stars', so the mental traveller—like certain artists—puts him or herself in situations that are initially incomprehensible in order to perceive what it surely means to be human. Or, as with another metaphor of Socrates from the Platonic *Phaedo* where he tells of how, if all the string instruments in the world were destroyed, harmony would continue to exist in the *kosmos* as a system of ratio or proportion which is indestructible. It is that kind of audience which the genuine pedestrian is seeking and which he or she strongly wishes to attest.

For me, friendship is like that, the personal amity which comes from shared distance, of being in common situations which are totally unfamiliar and imperfect, whether geographic, social, or affective. It is the human affinity which occurs then—like the Socratic *form* of ideal harmony—that is the one sustaining and inerrant unity of our existence, supplementing our otherwise culpable exchanges.

It is that truth of potential worldly parity which indicates what we are *not* as private individuals but which is nevertheless secured from reciprocal earthly transience: the sole currency of ingenuous human life when we, in the presence of a companion and with tremendous effort, witness something entirely human that is without equivalence to anything that we—until that moment—know; something, in fact, akin to the metaphor of sexual union but on a far more immanent and engrained scale.

As a friend in Bidhada once said to me about his reforestation work, 'we can strike a stone an hundred times and it will not break, but then someone else comes along and hits the rock and it promptly splinters'. Our struggle towards understanding is sometimes like that and throughout periods of awful duress we often remain completely unaware of how we are actually proceeding forward in both phase and apprehension. All human residence and its variety of affection is always and only founded upon how it is that we have moved, move, and continue to move in time as well as place; yet, to paraphrase king Odysseus, the straw that we reap is often heavier than the grain.

~ On Friendship ~

IV ~ III

ULTIMATELY one's meticulous affinity for place and person might only find affective resolution in love that has no object; that is our final emotional destination or homecoming and our only true *nostos* and terminus.

To illustrate this kind of universal alliance let us look at a marble statue of a young Sakyamuni that is presently held by the Fogg Museum of Art in Cambridge, Massachusetts; a small figure, with an integral base which is presently on view in the gallery at the north-east corner of the building on the ground floor. It is dated to the late Sixth century of the Common Era, a time of the Northern Qia Sui Dynasty, and its origin is stated to be from Dingzhou in Hebei province. The piece was part of the Grenville Winthrop bequest.

The figure itself is about fourteen inches tall and possesses a fiery halo of about ten inches in height; the pedestal is of a similar measure. The model is made of white marble with polychromatic rendering in part except for the face and partially exposed chest both of which are finely polished almost to a degree of glazing. The head is firmly oval and uniformly convex and the ear-lobes are traditionally elongated; the curled or knotted hair has been painted an azure blue. Sakyamuni sits in a lotos pose with eyes closed and wears a crimson gown which is stained black in places; an undergarment is tied with a figure-of-eight knot at the sternum. His left hand rests upon his knee and a small dark globe is held between thumb and forefinger whilst his right hand is raised in the *abhaya mudra* or 'fear not gesture'. These latter fingers were once damaged but have been nicely repaired.

There is a great delicacy to the features of this image as the carving is masterful, exquisite, yet lightly precise and it is as if there is vitality and breath within the expression of both face and upper torso; so much minute movement is implied that the hard mineral quality of the stone assumes an internal, flickering, and numinous vitality. A patina come of time supplies the flesh on the upper abdomen with a pale and varying discolouration.

The young Sakyamuni—'the renouncer of the Sakya clan', a people living in the foothills of the Himalayas—is in a state of *dhyanayoga* or 'profound reflection', what is sometimes nowadays referred to as 'meditation' or 'prayer', when all thought or *ratio* is in suspense.

As one observes the perfectly animate yet thoroughly reposeful statue one becomes aware that there is no consciousness there within the psyche of the subject, for this *buddha* has been depicted by a master sculptor in a condition of deep mental or spiritual stability in which all individuality has been resolved and elided: this is a state of disembodied and absolute consciousness of the order of unconditional *quietus*. What the artist has carved is not so much the bodily outline and dress of his subject but more the unearthly and interior quality of his thought, or rather, the absence or negation of thought. To do this is extremely difficult for a craftsman and this is no stock item of sculpture, it is not a replica of a standard pattern and this is no copy but a unique model itself, entirely and perfectly ideal.

The artist has not simply portrayed the Sakyamuni in a situation of *dhyanayoga* from a worldly or outwardly sensible point of view for he has with this uncanny work and its terrific mastery of minute detail managed to make explicit the actual psychic or spiritual experience of this youthful *buddha*. What is represented is an annulment or submission of consciousness or that which has been achieved by the effort of enlightenment. There is no active witness apart from the sculptor and the viewer of the object for the figure has—in terms of its consciousness—paradoxically removed itself from terrestrial and diurnal life. This is a masterpiece not only of sculpture but also of human experience.

What is captured by this material character is a state of mentally being without word, of being simultaneously detached from all bodily sensation and practice, including the breath and fluctuation of an undulant diaphragm and the *tempo* and rhythmic tide of the heart. This is a condition of being that is without bliss for there is neither *ecstasy* nor joyous illumination occurring: no one is there as the *buddha* has succeeded in removing awareness from his corporeal dimension and imperative—particularly the emotional and the verbal—and has calmed his physiological currency so that he is actually paused in gentle *stasis*, eschewing all cadence.

Consciousness here is thus foregone and has been replaced with that cosmic activity which informs all earthly life and being; this is the perfect equilibrium of the universe and of all its million-fold elements and components. It is as if the statue does not exist and what is present is merely a sign or *simulacrum* of such negation, an infinitely bare shell; yet the deficiency is one in which there is a completely full integrity of the *kosmos* with its formal unity and lack of distinction.

The sculptor has managed to represent something which can never become humanly apparent—not in our sublunary and conscious terms—for this young *buddha* has extinguished his psyche to a phenomenal situation where there is a totality that is impartial and thoroughly mediate: an equal union of both illusion and emptiness or that primary charge and principle which impels creation and lies at the heart of our presence and perception. It is from this condition that all else emanates, becoming ultimately the nature of language in its acoustic, visual, and mental qualities, our emotional and affective kind and the true nature of being aware, one that is without instrumentality or cause.

Friendship—as an affective medium of human existence—whether it be directed at the subtlety of landscape and such a revelatory awareness, or whether it concern a trustworthy relation with animals or birds; whether it is expressed in double form between two individuals who determine to share time, thought, words, inward experience, and perhaps bodily stimulation and sensation, or whether it is ultimately focused upon an awareness or conception of the universe itself, is always an outline of reciprocity: for nothing is inanimate if we pay attention to it and if we are generous in our comprehension of indebtedness; and that is mysterious.

If we do not exist in a commonwealth of attention and understanding we do not exist, for altruism is the unveiling principle of such quotidian life. Developing our consideration of a terrain, just as with the effort and attention required to comprehend the manners and being of a friend, are something to which I have devoted much of my life and such dedication has supplied me with my fortune.

As with friends, I think of places that I have loved and passed time with and their wonderful, beautiful, and most revealing expressions long after I have left them. Yet ultimately it is love that has no object which is the only firm and true companion and destination in this living world and how it is that we capture and are captivated by what lies beyond a situation, which sustains us in time. The multitudinous efficiency of friendship is the agency which first qualifies us for life and, given the awkwardness and inconcinnity of so much contemporary urban modernity, this kind of attachment is all that we might claim as a ground for intimacy in our various swerving and sometimes reckless ways; friendship partakes of the model of heroism, in that sense. If landscape is the perfect messenger, so too is the absent friend, that one who is always resident in our hearts and whom we think about frequently.

To be continued

~ On Friendship ~

ANIMAEEVOLUT

IONGRIEFRECIP

IENCETERRAINB

EAUTYMORALA

MBULATIONELE

CTIONCOOPER

ATIONFRIENDS

HIPPSYCHE

ACKNOWLEDGMENTS

I ~ III was printed in part in the Keats-Shelley Review, Vol. 17, 2003.
A short version appeared in the Harvard Magazine as, *A Romantic Swim*,
Spring, 2002.

II ~ II in short form was printed in, *Temenos Academy Review*, 6, 2004.

A version of III ~ I was printed in, *The Harvard Review*, 44, 2014.

III ~ II in short form was printed in, *Temenos Academy Review*, 18, 2016.

An early version of III ~ III appeared in,
In The Kacch, MacFarland, NC, 2014.

IV ~ I was printed in *Temenos Academy Review*, 25, 2023

ABOUT THE AUTHOR

Kevin McGrath was born in southern China in 1951 and was educated in England and Scotland; he has lived and worked in France, Greece, and India. Presently he is an Associate of the Department of South Asian Studies and Poet Laureate at Lowell House, Harvard University.
Publications include, *Fame* (1995); *Lioness* (1998); *The Sanskrit Hero* (2004); *Flyer* (2005); *Comedia* (2008); *Stri* (2009); *Jaya* (2011); *Supernature* (2012), *Heroic Krsna* and *Eroica* (2013); *In The Kacch* and *Windward* (2015); *Arjuna Pandava* and *Eros* (2016); *Raja Yudhisthira* (2017); *Bhisma Devavrata* (2018); *Vyasa Redux* (2019); *Song Of The Republic* (2020); *Fame* (2023); and *Causality In Homeric Song* (forthcoming 2024).
McGrath lives in Cambridge, Massachusetts, with his family.

Typefaces Used

Lucida Calligraphy
GILL SANS – Gill Sans
GARAMOND – Garamond
PERPETUA TITLING MT – PERPETUA TITLING